D1420415

000002151549

Rocking the System

Rocking the System

Fearless and Amazing Irish Women who Made History

Siobhán Parkinson

Little
Island

Rocking the System
First published in 2017 by
Little Island Books
7 Kenilworth Park
Dublin 6W
Ireland

ISBN: 978-1-910411-96-4

A British Library Cataloguing in Publication record for this book is available from the British Library.

Illustrated by Bren Luke
Design by Fidelma Slattery

Printed in Poland by Drukarnia Skleniarz

Little Island receives financial assistance from The Arts Council/An Chomhairle Ealaíon and the Arts Council of Northern Ireland

54321

Fellow Rockers

I could not have written this book on my own. I owe a great debt to Celia Keenan, who kindly volunteered to chair a *Rocking the System* research committee. This committee helped me to select the women appearing in the book and provided information about them. Thank you to Roger Bennett, Gráinne Clear, Valerie Coghlan, Gerard Hynes, Helen Litton, Liz Morris, Orla Parkinson, Matthew Parkinson-Bennett and Olivia Parkinson Coombs. Thank you, Martin Maguire, for guidance on the historical content.

A special thank you also to the women who agreed to be interviewed: Lian Bell, Lelia Doolan, Garry Hynes, Sr Stanislaus Kennedy and Paula Meehan.

Siobhán Parkinson

Preface

Many girls growing up in Ireland today have hopes and dreams
that would have seemed impossible to their great-grandmothers
and their great-great-grandmothers. They can hope to go to
university. They can dream of becoming doctors or politicians
or great artists or renowned writers. They can aspire to one day
becoming mothers who also have careers outside of the home.
They can even dream of some day being President of Ireland.

It is easy to take such choice and opportunity for granted,
and to forget the many women who fought, with great deter-
mination, to create a more equal world. It took many years
and many hard battles and acts of courage to achieve a society
where women are allowed to vote, to own their own homes, to
study alongside men in our universities and colleges and to plan
futures of possibility and opportunity.

It is important, therefore, that we remember the women who
refused to accept a world where they were considered to be of
less importance, and to have fewer rights than men. They were

women who not only wanted a more equal world for themselves and other women, but a more equal world for all those who were poor or oppressed or treated with great injustice.

They were very determined women, who refused to be discouraged by the barriers that made it difficult for females to speak out and to make a real difference to the world around them. They were women who had to force and drive their way into parts of society where they were often not wanted and not welcome. But by not being afraid to do so, they gradually changed the shape of their society, pushing out its boundaries so that more people could fit in and take their place as equal citizens.

It is interesting that so many of the determined women who feature in this book were born into rich families and privileged lives. It would have been very easy for them to ignore the injustice and hardships that less fortunate people had to live with. But their generosity, compassion and sense of fairness did not allow them to do this. They did not want to live in a society where others were suffering unfairly, and so they, along with many more women, committed their lives to helping others and trying to create a better and more just world.

Many of the women in this book are long dead, but they made an important difference to the society we live in today. Many others are carrying on the vital work of breaking down barriers and using their skills and talent to make our world a place where all will be welcomed and equally respected.

Today, very few of us will be called upon to give up our lives or our freedom in the struggle for a fairer society. But we will all be challenged in our everyday lives, in our classrooms and in our places of work and in our communities, to stand up for people who are victims of injustice or unkindness. Many battles have been won by the brave women who went before us, and the unknown heroines who walked so quietly alongside them.

We owe a debt of gratitude to those women and must continue their fight in a world that faces new and difficult challenges.

We have much to learn from the women who have rocked, and continue to rock, the system. I hope this book will inspire all its readers to ensure that they, too, play their part in creating a society shaped to fit all its members, and a world that is fair, harmonious and equal.

Sabina Coyne Higgins.

October 2017

Introduction

There is an old saying that goes: 'The hand that rocks the cradle rules the world.' This is supposed to mean that women have all the power. (Yeah, right!) When Mary Robinson won the presidential election in 1990 and became Ireland's first female president, she said that the women of Ireland, in voting for a woman with her kinds of views, had, instead of rocking the cradle, 'rocked the system'. That is of course where we got the title for this book, which celebrates how Irish women have made a difference to Irish life over the years – and, in many cases, the centuries.

The Irish people voted for a woman to be President of Ireland in the last decade of the 20th century, but in the first decade of that century, having a woman in that kind of position would have been unthinkable. Women could not even vote at that time, not to mind become president. It is only because women like Countess Markievicz and Hanna Sheehy Skeffington fought so hard for it (along with suffragettes in Britain) that women got the vote in 1918. That was an important landmark in

Irish women's history, but the struggle for women's rights is still going on in modern Ireland.

Not all the women discussed in this book would think of themselves as feminists. But all of them, from Queen Medhbh, who led an army into battle, to Lady Gregory, who co-founded the Abbey Theatre, to Mainie Jellett, who introduced Ireland to Modernist art, to Sonia O'Sullivan, who is a record-breaking athlete, have done amazing things in their fields, and shown that women, like other humans, can achieve wonderful things. But very often they achieve these things in spite of the way the world is designed – mostly *by* and certainly *for* non-women.

There are politicians and artists, warriors and campaigners, creators and do-ers, rockers of cradles and non-mothers too in this book. All of them had to struggle, in one way or another, to achieve what they have achieved. Many of them are or were educated women who had the good fortune to come from privileged backgrounds. They were able to become politically active or pursue artistic ways of life mainly because they did not have to hold down jobs or bring up families on low incomes. Poorer women had and still have it much tougher. But even the most privileged among these women had to fight for what they wanted, simply because they were women and had lower status and less freedom than men. They are or were all brave and dedicated. The number of them who were imprisoned, for example, for their beliefs and political actions is remarkable.

We have taken a largely historical approach in this book and have chosen to include here women who have had full careers over the years and many achievements. Today's younger women will, we know, be appearing in books like this in future decades. We also look forward with great excitement to seeing women from immigrant communities that have arrived more recently in Ireland emerging as rockers of the system too.

Rock on, women. Ireland has need of you.

Queen Medhbh (Maeve)

c. 1st century BC

Queen Medhbh is a mythological warrior queen, an image of how Ireland represented female power in the ancient past

Medhbh (Maeve) was Queen of Connacht and a major character in Ireland's great epic *Táin Bó Cúailnge* (The Cattle Raid of Cooley). This story was written down in medieval times, but it is set several centuries earlier.

According to the *Táin*, Medhbh was the daughter of the High King of Ireland. She had five sisters. Medhbh boasted that she was the best: she outdid all her sisters in grace and generosity and fierceness in battle. The last part certainly seems to be true of the Medhbh we know from the *Táin*.

Medhbh and Ailill had seven sons and a daughter. Once, Medhbh asked her druid which of her sons would kill Conchobar, and he said 'Maine'. Since she didn't have a son called Maine, she just renamed them all Maine. They didn't have a say in the matter. One of her sons did go on to kill a man called Conchobar, but unfortunately for Medhbh it was not the Conchobar she had had in mind.

When she was a young woman, Medhbh's father gave her in marriage to Conchobar Mac Neasa (Conor Mac Nessa), King of Ulster. The marrriage did not last: Medhbh left Conchobar and went home to Tara.

Her father went on to conquer Connacht and set Medhbh up as queen there. This put her in a powerful position, of course. Men came from other kingdoms all over Ireland to ask for her hand in marriage, but she claimed she wouldn't have any of them. She would only marry a man whose wedding present to her would be to never be mean, jealous or cowardly. Her husband definitely would need not to be jealous, as Medhbh was not a woman to be faithful to a husband.

In any case, Medhbh went on to have several husbands. Eventually, she settled down, more or less, with Ailill Mac Mata.

Medhbh told Ailill that she could not have married a timid man – that would be all wrong, because she herself thrived on all kinds of trouble. She was certainly right about that. She went on to cause a fierce battle between her kingdom of Connacht and the kingdom of Ulster, which was ruled over by her first husband and now her mortal enemy, Conchobar Mac Neasa.

As Medhbh's husband, Ailill was made King of Connacht, but Queen Medhbh definitely wanted to be the boss in that royal family. She made this very clear to Ailill, saying that if anyone caused him trouble, she was the one who should get the compensation for any harm or injury to him, because she was the one who paid the bills. She was a woman who did not mince her words.

The real trouble started when Medhbh and Ailill got into an argument over who was wealthier. To settle it, they had all their treasures and possessions and herds of animals brought out and counted. It turned out that they were exactly equal in every way – except for the White Bull. According to the *Táin*, the White Bull had left Medhbh's herd and joined Ailill's instead, because it refused to be led by a woman. (Even the animals could be misogynists in ancient Ireland, it seems.)

Medhbh wanted a bull that would be better than the White Bull, so that she could outdo her husband. She found out that there was indeed a finer bull in the country. This was the Donn Cúailnge or the Brown Bull of Cooley. The Brown Bull was owned by a chieftain called Daire, in the kingdom of her old enemy Conchobar Mac Neasa, King of Ulster.

Medhbh had to have that bull! She sent messengers to ask for the loan of it so that she could win the contest with Ailill. Stupidly, the messengers offended the bull's owner by boasting that Medhbh could have taken the bull anyway by force if she wanted to. The deal was off.

Enraged, Medhbh raised an army from all over Ireland to invade Ulster and help her to carry off the prized Brown Bull.

> Medhbh persuaded Ferdia, Cú Chulainn's foster-brother and best friend, to fight Cú Chulainn. There followed a fierce combat between the two friends, which ended with Cú Chulainn killing his beloved foster-brother. The ford where this happened was called Áth Fherdia in his honour – known in English as Ardee.

Many kings came to fight on her side – which shows how much authority she had.

Now, the warriors of Ulster had a problem. Their kingdom was being invaded by Medhbh's army – but they were all in bed, in dreadful pain. They had forced the noblewoman Macha to run a race while she was heavily pregnant. As a punishment for this, Macha put a curse on them: they were to feel the pains of a woman in labour. They were certainly in no state to fight a battle.

There was a rule of combat at the time which allowed a champion to challenge an army to send out one warrior to fight him at a ford, to settle whether the army would be allowed to cross the ford. One Ulster warrior, Cú Chulainn, who was not affected by the curse, took advantage of this rule to keep Medhbh's army out of Ulster. Each day, he demanded that the army send out a warrior to fight him in single combat.

Medhbh sent warrior after warrior against Cú Chulainn. She offered each of them her daughter in marriage if they could beat Cú Chulainn. But nobody could defeat the great Ulster hero. All this single-combat fighting day by day delayed Medhbh's progress into Ulster, and bought time for the King of Ulster's army.

Eventually the rest of the warriors of Ulster recovered from their curse, and there was a great battle between Medhbh's army and the army of Ulster. Medhbh was not afraid to take part in the fighting herself. One Ulster warrior described how fierce she looked, standing tall and holding a sharp lance in

Women in Irish mythology

Irish mythology features many women in roles that would have been unthinkable for women in later centuries.

Macha outran the King of Ulster's horses, despite being nine months pregnant. She is remembered in the placename of Eamhain Mhacha (called Navan Fort in English) near Armagh (Ard Macha).

Scáthach was a skilled warrior who trained Ireland's greatest warrior hero, Cú Chulainn, who went on to defeat Queen Medhbh.

The Irish god of war is female: the goddess Morrígan often takes the form of a raven and appears on battlefields in Irish legend.

Children were usually given their father's name as a surname, but some notable people took their mother's name instead – for example, Conchobar Mac Neasa, King of Ulster, and Medhbh's later husband, Ailill Mac Mata.

one hand and a great iron sword in the other, with her rich purple cloak folded about her.

Medhbh lost the battle and finally had to make peace with the men of Ulster. Cú Chulainn chased Medhbh and eventually did catch up with her; but in the end he did not kill her, as he thought it wrong for a man to kill a woman.

It had taken the legendary fighting of Cú Chulainn and all the warriors of Ulster to defeat Medhbh. She was blamed for causing so much death and destruction. Fergus Mac Róich – previously King of Ulster, who had fought on Medhbh's side in the battle – complained that they had followed a woman who led them astray. He described the battle as being like a herd of horses led by a mare – it goes all over the place. The men of Ireland obviously did not much like having a woman in a position of authority in battle – not even (or perhaps especially not) one as bloodthirsty and powerful as Queen Medhbh of Connacht.

Even though she lost the battle, Medhbh still managed to get hold of the bull. She brought him back to Connacht. There followed a mighty fight between the White Bull and the Brown Bull. The White Bull was killed, and the Brown Bull also died later of his wounds.

According to some stories Medhbh eventually became jealous of Ailill for seeing other women, and she goaded a warrior called Conall Cernach into killing him. Years later, Medhbh was herself killed while bathing in Lough Ree. Her nephew Furbaide took revenge on her for killing his mother. She lived in violent times, when power was won by strength and cleverness – two things Queen Medhbh had plenty of.

Medhbh is of course a mythological figure rather than a historical person. We only know her from the stories that were told of her and that were later written down by scribes. Still, her stories give us some idea of the power women seem to have been able to wield in early Ireland, the prejudices they faced and the achievements they could accomplish.

Queen Medhbh

Fact File

SINCE Medhbh is a mythological figure we don't have any precise dates for her life. Some manuscripts claim that she ruled during the 1st century BC.

MEDHBH'S capital was the ringfort at Cruachan, now Rathcroghan in County Roscommon.

SHE gathered an army of kings and warriors from all over Ireland to capture Donn Cúailnge, the Brown Bull of Cooley.

SHE may have been a goddess in early Irish mythology and was only turned into a human queen by later (Christian) writers – but we don't know this for sure.

HER name may come from the same root as the word 'mead', meaning an alcoholic drink made from honey. Some say that this reflects her intoxicating personality.

ACCORDING to some stories she is buried under the stone cairn on the summit of Knocknarea, County Sligo. Other stories claim she is buried at her capital, Rathcroghan in Roscommon.

THERE are various old manuscripts that contain versions or parts of the story of the *Táin*, and the story we know has been jigsawed together from the different manuscripts. Two of these manuscripts, The Yellow Book of Lecan and The Book of Leinster, are in Trinity College Dublin, and The Book of the Dun Cow is in the Royal Irish Academy in Dublin.

THE *Táin* has been translated many times into English. Two of the most recent translations are by the poets Thomas Kinsella and Ciaran Carson, and these books are easily available. There is a simplified *Táin* story for children by Liam Mac Uistin, published in Dublin by The O'Brien Press.

Gráinne Ní Mháille (Granuaile)

c. 1530–c. 1693

Gráinne Ní Mháille (or Grace O'Malley, nicknamed Granuaile) was an iconic Gaelic leader at a time of political chaos in Ireland

Gráinne Ní Mháille has long been commemorated in song and folklore as Granuaile. But her place in formal Irish history was barely acknowledged before the 20th century. She was a powerful leader who 'surpassed the part of womanhood' (as the Lord Justice of Ireland at the time, Sir William Drury, said of her). She had a fleet of galleys (ships powered by oarsmen as well as sails) at her disposal. The most amazing thing is that men were prepared to fight under her command.

The Tudors (King Henry VIII and after him Queen Elizabeth I) had decided that the conquest of Ireland needed to be completed. Their method was to divide and conquer. They stirred up strife among Irish chieftains and clans. In the face of this, Granuaile held on to her family's lands and their power at sea through her astuteness as a political leader, her prowess as a sea captain and her fierceness as a fighter.

Gráinne Ní Mháille was the daughter of a Gaelic chieftain whose home territory overlooked Clew Bay in County Mayo. Her family's territory included the islands in Clew Bay as well as onshore lands known as the Umhall Uachtar. They had a strong

The Brehon Laws, the ancient legal system of Ireland, were still in force in parts of Ireland in Gráinne Ní Mháille's day. These laws did not treat women as equal to men, but they did allow women to own and inherit property. This was not the usual thing in other countries. They also allowed women to divorce their husbands in certain circumstances.

However, a woman could not become a chieftain. Gráinne behaved as a chieftain but she was not legally entitled to be called one.

Granuaile

Gráinne Ní Mháille is usually known by the nickname Granuaile. There is a story that, as a girl, Gráinne cut off all her hair so that she could go seafaring with her father, like a boy. The story goes that she was called Gráinne Mhaol (Gráinne the Bald) because of that haircut. This is supposed to be the origin of the name Granuaile.

However, it is likely that the nickname actually comes from Gráinne Umhaill (pronounced oo-ai), meaning Gráinne of Umhall, since that was the area of land owned by her family, which she inherited.

seafaring tradition, and most of their income came from the sea. They undertook regular trading voyages around the coast of Ireland, to Scotland and to Spain. There is no doubt that they were also pirates and plunderers.

As a young woman, Gráinne broke with convention and went to sea with her father. She learned seafaring skills that women were not usually allowed to learn.

When she was sixteen she married Dónal Ó Flatharta,

In Gráinne Ní Mháille's time, Irish chieftains did not automatically inherit their titles from their father. Various men of the clan could be eligible to become chieftain, any one of whom might be elected *tánaiste* (heir).

known as Dónal an Chogaidh (Donal the Warlike), who was in line to be chieftain of the O'Flahertys of County Clare. She and Dónal had three children.

Dónal was killed in a feud with a neighbouring family. According to Irish law at the time, Gráinne was entitled to get her dowry back on the death of her husband, along with some of his property. It is not clear that she got all she was due, but she inherited wealth from her mother too, and her father's very prosperous seafaring business also passed to her. Over time, she became a rich woman.

After her husband died, Gráinne moved back to her own family's territory. Many of her late husband's fighting men left their home area and followed her back to Mayo. She set herself up in an O'Malley castle on Clare Island. From there she ran her family's seafaring and trading operations. Any ships that entered Clew Bay had to pay tolls or taxes to the O'Malleys, and if they did not pay up, they might be murdered. This amounted to piracy, which was strictly illegal, but also quite common.

There is a story that Gráinne, hearing of a boat in trouble near Achill island, set off to see what she could salvage from the wreckage. She rescued a young man who had been washed onto some rocks. He would have died if Gráinne had not saved him. His name was Hugh de Lacy, and he and Gráinne fell in love.

The romance did not last long, because Hugh was killed soon afterwards by a local family. Gráinne was not long tracking down his murderers and taking her revenge by killing them in her turn. She was a fierce woman.

About a year after her first husband's death, Gráinne remarried. Her second husband was Richard Bourke, nicknamed Risteard an Iarainn (Iron Richard – probably because of his family's ironworks). He was from a powerful family and looked likely to inherit the chieftainship of his clan one day and become The MacWilliam Bourke – the highest title in Connacht. He also owned castles in Mayo that would be convenient for Gráinne's purposes.

Gráinne had one son by her marriage to Richard. His name was Tibbot or Tiobóid Bourke, and he was known as Tiobóid na Long (Tibbot of the Ships) because he was born at sea. The story is told that Gráinne was lying with her baby in her arms the day after he was born when her ship was attacked, and the sailors begged her to get up and help them to fight off the enemy. She got up and killed several of the corsairs who were attacking her ship.

Another story says that after a year of marriage, Gráinne divorced Richard. She did this by locking him out of his castle and calling out 'Richard Bourke, I dismiss you' to him from the battlements of the castle. However, it looks as if Gráinne changed her mind about divorcing Richard, because they were still married years later. All the same, she never gave the castle back, and she went on living there for most of the rest of her life. It is called

Carraig an Chabhlaigh (Carrigahowley or Rockfleet Castle in English) and is still standing. It is near Newport in County Mayo.

English law was in force in many parts of Ireland, but Connacht was one of the areas that held out the longest against the English. Queen Elizabeth I was afraid that the Irish would link up with Catholic Spain, England's great enemy at the time. Partly for that reason, she wanted to bring Ireland under English rule. Her plan was to get Irish chieftains to acknowledge her as queen of the 'Kingdom of Ireland'. In return she would let them keep their lands and would give them English titles.

There was a lot of unrest and fighting in Connacht over many years around this time. Granuaile played along with the English up to a point, when it suited her. Her husband Richard Bourke did a deal with the English in 1581 and was knighted. Richard died soon afterwards, but Gráinne's struggle against English power went on for decades.

Sir Richard Bingham was Queen Elizabeth's main representative in Connacht. His job was to enforce English rule and keep the Irish chieftains down. Granuaile supported Irish lords in their rebellions against the Crown. She was captured by Bingham and imprisoned in Dublin Castle. Bingham wanted to have her hanged, but her son-in-law offered himself as a hostage in her place and she was freed. Bingham's brother murdered Gráinne's eldest son, Eoin, and some years later Bingham imprisoned Gráinne's other two sons and her half-brother.

After corresponding with Queen Elizabeth about this, Gráinne decided that the best thing was to go and meet the queen face to face. Even though she was by now quite an old woman, by the standards of the time, Gráinne set off and sailed right up the Thames to Greenwich. It was not easy to get to see the queen. But Elizabeth, as a woman in a man's world herself, was intrigued to meet this Irishwoman who commanded armies and fleets.

The Spanish Armada

A huge fleet of warships from Spain, known as the Spanish Armada, attacked England in 1588. There were terrible storms that year, and many of the ships were wrecked off the Irish coasts. Sir Richard Bingham ordered that all survivors from the ships were to be executed, which they mostly were.

It seems that one of these ships came to grief off Clare Island in Granuaile's territory. Apparently about a hundred survivors came ashore on the island. Bingham reported back to the queen that the islanders had killed them.

If this massacre did take place (and it is not clear if it did), it was probably a kinsman of Gráinne's that was involved. She seems not to have been on the island at the time.

> Gráinne was of course an Irish speaker and Elizabeth spoke English. They were both educated women and had studied Latin, and it is said that they spoke in Latin at their meeting. But it is not all that likely, as Latin would mostly have been used for written documents.
>
> Gráinne probably knew some English; and Elizabeth could have had some Irish. She was a good linguist and spoke many languages. We will never know how they conversed, but it could have been in a mixture of languages and there would also have been interpreters at court.

After a lot of discussion, Elizabeth agreed to remove Bingham from his position in Connacht and to free Gráinne's family members. In return, Gráinne was not to support the Irish lords who were in rebellion against English law.

Gráinne's sons and brother were released and Bingham was removed. But very soon afterwards Bingham was sent to Connacht again. When Elizabeth broke her bargain, Gráinne went back to supporting rebellion in Connacht.

For most of her life, Gráinne Ní Mháille was involved in conflict – in piracy, fighting, rebellion. But she also knew how to make bargains and negotiate settlements. She was one of the last of the Gaelic clan rulers and military leaders – and the only one we know of who was female. Ireland eventually came under full English rule after the Battle of Kinsale, shortly before Gráinne's death. She is believed to have died in 1603, the same year as her adversary, Queen Elizabeth.

Granuaile's son Tiobóid na Long went on to inherit his father's title as The MacWilliam Bourke and was later made a viscount (a kind of lord) by Elizabeth. There is still a Lord Mayo, a distant cousin of the original family.

Granuaile

Fact File

c. 1530 Born the only child of her parents (though her father also had a son by another relationship, Gráinne's half-brother, Dónal na bPíob).

1546 Married Dónal an Chogaidh Ó Flatharta, *tánaiste* (elected heir) to the O'Flaherty chieftainship of Iar-Chonnacht (roughly modern-day Connemara); there were three children of this marriage: Eoin, Muircheadha (Murrough) and Maighréad.

1565 Her husband Dónal killed in a feud.

1566 Married Richard Bourke, who went on to inherit one of the most important titles in the whole of Connacht.

1567 Her son Tióbóid na Long born at sea, only child of her second marriage.

1576 Granuaile made peace with Sir Henry Sidney, the lord deputy of Ireland.

1577 Granuaile plundered the lands of the Earl of Desmond, was captured by him and kept a prisoner until 1579.

Granuaile

Fact File

1581 Gráinne's second husband, Richard Bourke, knighted; died soon afterwards.

1584 Richard Bingham made governor of Connacht; controversy, conflict and chaos followed, which lasted for decades.

1586 Gráinne captured by Bingham and imprisoned in Dublin Castle; released when her son-in-law offered himself as a hostage in her place.

1586 Gráinne's eldest son, Eoin, murdered by Bingham's brother.

1588 Spanish Armada wrecked off the coast of Ireland.

1593 Gráinne's two surviving sons and her half-brother imprisoned by Sir Richard Bingham; Gráinne visited Queen Elizabeth I; managed to get her family members out of prison and get rid of Bingham, but he was soon reinstated.

c. 1603 Died.

Eibhlín Dubh Ní Chonaill

c. 1743–*c.* 1800

Eibhlín Dubh Ní Chonaill wrote the greatest Irish poem of the 18th century, 'Caoineadh Airt Uí Laoghaire' ('A Lament for Art O'Leary')

Eibhlín Dubh Ní Chonaill (Dark-haired Eileen O'Connell) was a widow at the age of fifteen. She came from a wealthy family, and it is likely that her marriage was arranged. Eibhlín's husband was much older, and she was probably not very happy to marry him. He died just a few months after the wedding.

Some years later, Eibhlín fell head over heels in love with a handsome young rapscallion called Art Ó Laoghaire. Art had been educated abroad and served as a captain in the Hungarian Hussars. He liked to swagger around in fashionable clothes, wearing his sword – which Catholics were not allowed to do in those days.

Eibhlín's family did not approve of Art Ó Laoghaire. Maybe they did not like that he was proud and showy. Or it could be that they were afraid he was a trouble-maker. He was very much against the way the Penal Laws were used against Catholics like himself in his home area of North Cork.

This time, though, Eibhlín was going to marry the man she loved. For a young woman from an upper-class family to elope was unthinkable at that time, but that is what Eibhlín did.

> There is a legend that when Eibhlín came to live in her first husband's house, the strings on the harp in the hall broke – a sign of bad luck. It is also said that Eibhlín sat cracking nuts all night at her husband's wake – which sounds as if she was not very sad about his death.

Eibhlín's husband, Art Ó Laoghaire, had an enemy, a local magistrate called Abraham Morris. Morris was part of the establishment in the area, which enforced the Penal Laws very fiercely against Catholics. The dispute between the two men went on over about two years.

One morning, Art left his house, after kissing Eibhlín and his two little boys goodbye, and he never came back. His horse

Art defies the Penal Laws

The Penal Laws oppressed people who did not belong to the Established (Anglican) church. This included Presbyterians, for example. But the people affected by these laws in most parts of Ireland were Catholics, the majority of the native Irish population. For example, only Anglicans could be soldiers or magistrates or hold any position of authority. The Penal Laws were harshly enforced by the legal authorities and others in power at that time in north Cork.

The law said that a Catholic could not own a horse worth more than £5. If a magistrate offered him that amount, the Catholic had to sell the horse. Abraham Morris, who was a magistrate, offered Art Ó Laoghaire £5 for his horse. Art refused. This gave Morris an excuse to harass and persecute Art.

Later Morris accused Art of seizing his gun. Art admitted that he did take the gun, but he said he acted in self-defence. Morris tried to make out that this made Art an outlaw.

came home riderless and covered in blood. Eibhlín knew immediately that her husband had been shot. She jumped up on the bloody mare and went riding off to find him. This was not the kind of thing that a lady of Eibhlín's class did in 1773. But Eibhlín Dubh was an independent and passionate woman, and she did as she chose.

Eibhlín found the body of her beloved husband where it lay at Carraig an Ime, near their family home at Macroom, and launched into a lament for him. She says in the poem that, instead of cleaning up his blood, she drank it from her hands. It is said that she later shot the mare in a fit of rage at Art's death. The horse is buried under the stable yard at Art and Eibhlín's home, Rathleigh House.

The oral (spoken) lament that Eibhlín began when she found Art's body was later expanded into a long dramatic poem, known as 'Caoineadh Airt Uí Laoghaire'. The poem is not written in the kind of language that you would expect from a lady at that time. By mourning her husband loudly and fiercely and calling for revenge, Eibhlín is doing what women of her class at that time were not supposed to do. She calls down curses on the murderer's head. And she does not call for someone else to avenge Art's death – she talks of doing it herself.

As well as being a personal expression of grief and anger, 'Caoineadh Airt Uí Laoghaire' is a political poem, in which the widow is not afraid to name the man who murdered her husband. It is also valuable as a record of the Gaelic way of life, which at the time it was written was coming to an end.

'Caoineadh Airt Uí Laoghaire' is more than a great Irish poem. According to Declan Kiberd, a well-known professor of Irish literature, it is 'one of the great elegies of European culture'. The English poet and academic Peter Levi called it 'the greatest poem written in these islands in the whole 18th century' – which is high praise indeed for a poem written in a minority language by a woman with no training as a poet.

Modern translations of the poem

Dear Art,
when you passed through the gate
it didn't take you long
to turn back
to kiss your fine sons
and your airy wife,
to leave these words
on her tongue forever:
'Eileen, look lively,
steady yourself.
I am leaving the house
and I might not be back.'

from Vona Groarke's translation, Lament for Art O'Leary

I leaped across my bed
I leaped then to the gate
I leaped upon your mare
I clapped my hands in frenzy
I followed every sign
With all the skill I knew
Until I found you lying
Dead beside a furze bush ...

from Brendan Kennelly's translation, 'A Cry for Art O'Leary'

Eibhlín Dubh Ní Chonaill

Fact File

c. 1743 The exact year of Eibhlín Dubh's birth is not clear but it was around 1743; she was born into a wealthy family, the O'Connells of Derrynane, County Kerry, and was one of twenty-two children.

EIBHLÍN Dubh was an aunt of the great Irish parliamentarian Daniel O'Connell the Liberator, who secured Catholic Emancipation in 1829.

AT the age of fifteen she married a man called O'Connor, who was many years older than she was; she was widowed within months.

1767 She fell in love with and married Captain Art Ó Laoghaire and went to live with him at his family home, Rathleigh House, in Macroom, County Cork.

EIBHLÍN and Art had two sons (as well as other children who died as babies).

1771 Abraham Morris offered Art Ó Laoghaire £5 for his horse; Art refused; later that year Art was charged with various crimes, including seizure of a gun belonging to Abraham Morris, for which he was never tried; Morris offered

Eibhlín Dubh Ní Chonaill

Fact File

a reward for the capture of Art, although he was not in fact an outlaw.

1773 Art Ó Laoghaire was shot dead near his home in Macroom; Abraham Morris was at first found guilty of his murder but later acquitted; Eibhlín Dubh, on discovering her beloved husband's body, composed the opening lines of her famous lament.

THERE were legal problems about burying Art's body at Kilcrea Friary in County Cork, where the family wanted him buried; there

had to be a temporary burial until that was sorted out. Not much is known about Eibhlín's life after this, though she may have gone to London to seek justice from the king.

c. 1800 The death of Eibhlín Dubh probably took place just as the 18th century became the 19th.

1892 It is not known when Eibhlín's poem was first written down, but it was not printed until 1892, in a book called *The Last Colonel of the Irish Brigade* by the wife of one of the O'Connell family.

Anne Devlin

c. 1778–1851

Anne Devlin
endured torture and
imprisonment rather
than betray Robert
Emmet and his comrades
to the authorities,
yet her role in history
has been consistently
undervalued

Anne Devlin was a cousin of Michael Dwyer, who fought in the rising of 1798. After the rising Michael went on the run, hiding out in the Wicklow mountains. Anne's immediate family did not take part in the rising. Even so, Anne's father was arrested and imprisoned without charge. He was left to languish for two and a half years in Wicklow Gaol, which was notorious for its harsh conditions. Anne brought supplies to her father twice a week – food, wine, clean shirts and sheets. He was eventually acquitted and re-leased in 1801.

Robert Emmet's older brother had fought in the 1798 rising and afterwards fled to America. Robert Emmet was determined to continue his brother's fight. He was planning a new rising, but he needed a safe place in the Dublin area from which to organise it. A cousin of Anne's called Arthur Devlin was friendly with Emmet. He helped him to find a suitable house in Butterfield Lane in Rathfarnham.

Anne agreed to act as Emmet's housekeeper, to make it look like a normal household. But she wasn't ever really a housekeeper and she was not paid by Emmet. She was close to the conspirators: Emmet described her as 'one of our own'.

> Two men who were executed for their part in the 1798 rising were buried in Leitrim graveyard in County Wicklow. Some people wanted their bodies moved from there and re-buried alongside their comrades in a different graveyard. The local men thought this would be too dangerous. So Anne and two of Michael Dwyer's sisters decided to do it themselves. They had two coffins made, and they dug up and moved the bodies in the dead of night.

She carried messages between Emmet and her cousin Michael Dwyer in Wicklow, but in the end Michael and his followers did not support Emmet's rising.

The rising took place in July 1803 but it was a dismal failure. The conspirators fled back to Butterfield Lane. Anne greeted them with these words: 'Oh, bad welcome to you, you cowards, is the world lost by you that you are to lead the people to destruction and then to leave them?'

When soldiers came looking for Robert Emmet in Rathfarnham, he had already gone to Wicklow. They tried to force Anne to give information about 'Mr Ellis' (Emmet's alias). They prodded her with bayonets, and then half-hanged her, but she would not tell them anything.

Robert Emmet came back to Dublin from Wicklow about a month after the rising, because he wanted to see his fiancée, Sarah Curran. He was arrested by Town-Major Sirr, the Chief of Police.

Anne and other members of her family were arrested and sent to Kilmainham Gaol. She met Emmet briefly in the prison yard. He urged her to save herself, because she could not save him anyway. But Anne would not give away any of the conspirators. She refused an offer of £500 from Major Sirr if she would give information. Emmet was executed shortly afterwards, along with twenty-one other conspirators.

By Christmas 1803, twenty-two members of Anne Devlin's family were in Kilmainham Gaol, including ten of the Dwyer family. Even Anne's youngest brother, Jimmy, aged seven, was imprisoned. He died soon afterwards of scarlet fever.

Anne was threatened with death by fellow prisoners. She lay on damp straw on a cold, wet earthen floor. She got a serious infection called erysipelas because of the terrible conditions. She did not get any medical treatment.

From Anne Devlin's *Jail Journal*

My father had some time before sent over to Mr
Emmet's residence a light cart to help give the
appearance of business. This they put standing up,
a rope was put over it and about my neck. ... I was
hauled over and the rope was thrown across the back
band. They shouted again, 'Will you tell now where
Mr Ellis is?'

'No, villains, I will tell you nothing about him,' I
said. I thought of praying and had only time to say,
'Oh, Lord, have mercy on me,' when they gave a
tremendous shout and pulled me up.

How long they kept me suspended I cannot say, but
at last I felt a kind of consciousness of my feet again
touching the ground. Their savage shouting had not
ceased at this time, and I felt a hand loosening the
rope on my neck.

Anne later wrote about her time in prison, 'After one year, if my spirits were still buoyant, want of exercise, bad diet and other ill-usages were making gradual inroad on my constitution.' Mrs Dunn, wife of the chief prison officer, befriended Anne, and often smuggled her into the Dunns' living quarters to clean her and feed her. She became one of Anne's best friends: 'I owe her a great debt of gratitude,' Anne wrote.

The law changed in Ireland in 1806, and it became illegal to keep people in prison without trial. Anne's father and other family members were let out of prison.

However, Edward Trevor, medical inspector of Kilmainham Gaol, was still determined to make Anne speak. He moved her to Dublin Castle. Here she was imprisoned in a window-less broom closet, so small that she could barely lie down. She was by now almost blind from the erysipelas. Mrs Hanlon, the widow of a former governor of the castle, found her by accident. She made sure Anne was finally released.

Anne had paid a heavy price for her loyalty to Emmet and the United Irishmen. She did recover from the worst effects of her prolonged imprisonment, and lived a fairly normal life for many years. She married and had children and worked as a laundress in St Patrick's Hospital, Dublin. However, she was always openly followed by the police, and anyone talking to her could be arrested.

In her later years, Anne was befriended by Dr Richard Madden, a historian of the 1798 United Irishmen rising. He encouraged her to write her *Jail Journal*.

After her husband's death, Anne fell on hard times and died in terrible poverty. She was buried with her husband, but Dr Madden, thinking she should be buried somewhere more important, dug up her coffin one night and moved it to a grave near the Daniel O'Connell monument in Glasnevin Cemetery.

From Anne Devlin's *Jail Journal*

After my liberation, in the latter end of 1806,
I frequently met with some of the former state
prisoners in the streets; they passed on without
seeming to recognise me. But something like an
inward agitation was visible on their countenance.
And although I may say I was then houseless
and friendless, I never troubled a being of them,
or anyone else with my distress, although I held
the life's thread of more than fifty of the most
respectable of them in my hands. But the pride
of acting right consoled me, and I never took into
account my incarceration, loss of health, the long
and wasting confinement, and destruction of my
whole family.

Here he erected a tombstone with the following inscription:

To the memory of Anne Devlin Campbell
The faithful servant of Robert Emmet
Who possessed some rare and many noble qualities
Who lived in obscurity and poverty
And so died on the 18th day of Sept. 1851,
aged 70 years.
May she rest in peace, Amen.

Anne Devlin

Fact File

c. **1778** Born to Bryan Devlin (possibly a house builder) and Winnie (née Byrne) in Cronebeg, near Aughrim, County Wicklow, one of a family of seven.

REARED as a Catholic, Anne grew up speaking and reading English, and also studied arithmetic; she was an excellent horsewoman.

1790s Family moved to Corballis, near Rathdrum, County Wicklow.

1798 The United Irishmen (an organisation mostly of Catholics and Presbyterians that was influenced by the French Revolution), led by Theobald Wolfe Tone, had a rising that was ultimately quashed; Robert Emmet's older brother fought in this rising, as did Anne Devlin's cousin Michael Dwyer.

1798 Anne's father was arrested and imprisoned, even though he had not been involved in the rising.

1799 Anne helped Michael Dwyer's sisters to dig up two bodies of rebels and re-bury them in a different graveyard.

1801 Anne's father released from Wicklow Gaol; family moved to Rathfarnham near Dublin.

1803 Anne acted as Robert Emmet's 'housekeeper' but was really involved in planning a new rising.

1803 Emmet's rising took place on 23 July and failed miserably; Anne tortured but refused to reveal whereabouts of Emmet; she and many of her family arrested and sent to Kilmainham Gaol.

Anne Devlin

Fact File

1803 Robert Emmet arrested in August and executed in September.

1806 Anne moved to Dublin Castle; rest of her family released from prison.

1806–10 After being released from imprisonment, went to work as a lady's companion to a Mrs Hammond of Rogerson's Quay, Dublin, until that lady's death.

1811 Married William Campbell, a drayman (driver of a type of cart used mostly to transport beer barrels).

WILLIAM and Anne lived in John's Lane in the centre of Dublin and had at least four children; Anne worked for many years as a laundress in St Patrick's Hospital.

1846 Anne's husband, William, died.

WITHOUT her husband's income, and without his cart to collect and deliver laundry, and with declining sight, Anne fell into poverty.

1851 Moved to Little Elbow Lane, off Meath Street, the worst slum in Dublin; six months later she died alone, starving and in agony.

THE cave-like cell with one tiny window and an earthen floor, where Anne Devlin was imprisoned for three years, can still be seen in Kilmainham Gaol in Dublin.

Anna Parnell

1852–1911

Anna Parnell, a pioneering
feminist, was leader of the
Ladies' Land League, the
first political association in
Ireland led by women

Anna Parnell was a leading political activist on behalf of tenant farmers in the late 19th century. At that time, almost all land in Ireland was owned by a small number of landlords. Tenant farmers had to pay rent to their landlord and they had no say in what was a reasonable rent. It was easy for landlords to evict people who did not pay up.

> 'If the Irish landlords had not deserved extermination for anything else, they would have deserved it for their treatment of their own women.'
>
> *Anna Parnell*

There was a lot of friction between landlords and tenants, especially in years when farmers could not pay their rent because of a bad harvest.

Even though Anna was from the landlord class, she was on the side of the tenants. The same was true of her famous brother Charles Stewart Parnell, who was a Member of Parliament (MP), and her sister Fanny, who was a poet. They were all nationalists, which means they thought that Ireland should not be ruled by Britain.

Anna's father died when she was seven. After that, the family moved around a lot, living in Paris, London and New Jersey (USA) as well as at Avondale, the Parnell family home, in County Wicklow. Anna did not have a formal education but, according to her brother John, she knew every book in the family library. She was good at painting and studied at the Royal Dublin Academy of Art and the Heatherly School of Art in London.

At that time, it was very difficult for women to take part in public life. They were not allowed to vote, never mind stand for election themselves. If they attended a political meeting, they had to sit in a gallery. When her brother Charles was elected to parliament in 1875, Anna, who at that stage was studying art in London, became a parliamentary correspondent for the

From 'Hold the Harvest'

The serpent's curse upon you lies – you writhe within the dust
You fill your mouths with beggars' swill, you grovel for a crust
Your masters set their blood-stained heels upon your shameful heads
Yet they are kind – they leave you still their ditches for your beds!

by Fanny Parnell
This poem urges Irish peasants to rebel.

> 'Everything recommended, attempted or done in the way of defeating the ordinary law and asserting the unwritten law of the League ... was more systematically carried out under the direction of the ladies' executive than by its predecessor.'
>
> *Michael Davitt*

Irish-American paper *Celtic Monthly*. She used to sit in the gallery and write irreverent articles called 'Notes from the Ladies' Cage'.

Anna became involved in politics in 1879, when the harvest failed and tenants could not pay their rents. Charles had become the leader of a new organisation called the Land League. The aim of this organisation was summed up in its slogan 'The land of Ireland for the people of Ireland'. Anna's sister Fanny set up an organisation in America to raise funds for poverty-stricken tenants in Ireland – which it did very successfully.

The Land League protested against the landlords, but without using violence. Instead, they used tactics like delayed payment or even non-payment of unfair rents, mass protests and obstructing evictions.

It became clear that members of the Land League were in danger of being imprisoned. Anna's sister Fanny thought it would be a good idea to set up a women's organisation to carry on the work of the Land League if this happened. Michael Davitt, one of the Land League leaders, was very impressed by the work done by the Parnell women in raising funds in America. He set up the Ladies' Land League in January 1881. He invited Anna Parnell to be its leader. The purpose of the Ladies' Land League was never properly communicated. The men probably thought that the women would just keep things ticking over while they were in prison.

The women had much more ambitious plans. The men were indeed imprisoned, and the women's organisation became more active. They challenged landlord rule and encouraged women to withhold rent and resist eviction. They support-ed evicted tenants and built huts for people who had been evicted. They were very effi-cient at administration. By July 1881 they had 420 branches and were providing help to over 3000 evicted people. They also established a Children's Land League so that boys and girls could be taught Irish history. And while they were doing all this, they supported the Land League men who were in prison, and arranged meals and other comforts for them.

> 'I think now that, added to their natural resentment at our having done what they asked us to do, they soon acquired a much stronger ground for their annoyance in the discovery that we were taking the Land League seriously and thought that not paying rent was intended to mean not paying it.'
>
> *from Anna Parnell's* Tale of a Great Sham

Conflict between landlords and tenants was at the centre of politics in Ireland at the time, and the Ladies' Land League was a major force in opposing unfair rents and landlords. The Ladies' Land League was a better-run organisation than the original Land League and achieved a great deal. Even so, it was very controversial. People did not approve of women abandon-ing their traditional roles and becoming politically active. The police often raided Ladies' Land League meetings, and some of the members were imprisoned. Unlike the men of the Land League, who were considered to be political prisoners, the women were treated as criminals.

> 'Perhaps when we are dead and gone and another generation grown up ... they will point to us as having set a noble example to all the women of Ireland.'
>
> *Anna Parnell*

When Charles Stewart Parnell was released from Kilmainham Gaol in April 1882, he set out to bring the Ladies' Land League firmly under male control. It was eventually dissolved, against the will of the women who were its leaders. The men went on to form the Irish National League to campaign on Home Rule. It was described as 'an open organisation in which the ladies will not take part'. Anna never spoke to her brother again.

The male version of Land League history is the one best known because Anna Parnell failed to get her account, *The Tale of a Great Sham*, published in her lifetime. It was rediscovered in 1959 but not published until 1986. That is how we now know more about what happened.

The Ladies' Land League was an important organisation in the political development of radical women. Women involved in the Ladies' Land League learned how to speak in public, to withstand criticism and ridicule and to run a national political organisation. Many of them went on to become involved in nationalist politics and in the suffragette movement.

Our knowledge of Anna's life after the Ladies' Land League came to an end is patchy. She lived in England for most of the time from 1886 until her death, as a recluse and under the assumed name of Cerisa Palmer. She did return to Ireland at least once during this time. In 1908 she travelled to Drumkeerin, County Leitrim, to support Sinn Féin in an election. When she tried to address the crowd, rotten eggs were thrown at her and a bucket of water was thrown over her.

She drowned in England in 1911.

Anna Parnell

Fact File

1852 Born at Avondale House in County Wicklow to a Protestant family.

ANNA'S mother Delia was American and had progressive ideas. Her daughters were brought up with more freedom than was usual in Irish families.

1859 Anna's father died and the family moved to Dublin and later to Paris and later still to New Jersey in the USA.

1870 Anna left home (Paris) and returned to Dublin to study art.

1870 On the outbreak of the Franco-Prussian war, Anna's sister Fanny and her mother joined the American Ladies' Committee in Paris and set up a hospital for soldiers.

1875 Anna became a parliamentary correspondent for the Irish-American paper *Celtic Monthly*.

1879 The Land League was founded, with Anna's brother Charles Stewart Parnell as its leader.

1880 The Ladies' Land League of New York was founded by Anna's sister, Fanny, to collect funds for impoverished Irish tenants.

1881 Michael Davitt set up the Ladies' Land League and Anna Parnell became its leader.

1882 Charles Stewart Parnell brought the Ladies' Land League under male control and eventually dissolved it, to Anna's disgust.

1886–1911 Anna lived in England under an assumed name.

1911 Anna drowned while swimming at Ilfracombe in Devon.

1986 *The Tale of a Great Sham*, Anna Parnell's angry account of her experience in the Ladies' Land League, edited by Dana Hearne, was published by Arlen House.

Augusta, Lady Gregory

1852–1932

Lady Gregory, writer, dramatist, theatre manager and folklorist, played an important role in the Irish Literary Revival of the late 19th and early 20th centuries

Lady Gregory is mostly known as a friend and patron of the poet WB Yeats as well as co-founder with him of the Abbey Theatre. But she was also a writer and dramatist in her own right. She wrote or translated nearly forty plays. She also published important collections of folklore and Irish mythology. She was a leading light in the Irish Literary Revival.

When she was a young woman, Augusta visited Egypt with her husband, who was much older than she was. There she met and fell in love with an Englishman called Wilfrid Scawen Blunt. She wrote a series of passionate love poems to him. She could not publish these under her own name, as she wanted to keep her love affair hidden. So she sent them to Wilfrid and said he could publish them as his own. This was the secret beginning of her life as a writer.

As well as being a landlord and politician, Augusta's husband, Sir William Gregory, was interested in languages and literature; his library at Coole was a great source of delight to Augusta. In the early years of their marriage, the Gregorys lived in London and Augusta hosted a literary salon. Guests included the novelist Henry James, the poet Robert Browning and the Poet Laureate, Lord Tennyson. But it was not until after William's death in 1892 that Augusta really began her writing career. A visit to the Aran Islands inspired her to study the Irish language. She went on to write versions of tales from the Ulster Cycle of Irish mythology (Cú Chulainn stories). It was partly because of her work in this area that these tales became more widely known.

She took a great interest in the speech of the local people who were her tenants. English as it is spoken in Ireland is usually known as Hiberno-English. But Lady Gregory called the dialect of English that the people around her spoke 'Kiltartanese', after the local townland of Kiltartan. She loved this form of English, which was heavily influenced by the Irish language. She

Sir William Gregory

The family Lady Gregory came from and the family she married into were very much part of the Anglo-Irish establishment and were loyal to the British Empire.

Lady Gregory's husband, Sir William Gregory, and his family prided themselves on being caring landlords. They tried to help the people during the Famine and they never evicted their tenants. Sir William was, however, responsible for a piece of legislation as an MP known as 'the Gregory clause'. This was not a good thing for poor people, and he never lived it down.

Lady Gregory herself took an interest in the tenants' welfare. She once set up a shop on the estate, because the local shopkeeper was over-charging. She charged lower prices, and we can guess that the local shopkeeper soon changed his tune.

Celtic Revival and Irish Literary Revival

Towards the end of the 19th century and into the early decades of the 20th, there was a great revival of interest in Gaelic culture – language, mythology, history, art, dance, music and games. Artists, scholars and writers became interested in Celtic art, Irish mythology and the Irish language. The Gaelic League (now Conradh na Gaeilge) and the GAA were founded late in the 19th century.

Hand-in-hand with this general Celtic Revival went a flowering of literary talent usually called the Irish Literary Revival. WB Yeats was the leading figure in the Literary Revival, which had its roots in meetings of poets and writers in Lady Gregory's house in Coole. Other important figures were JM Synge, Douglas Hyde, George Russell, Padraic Colum, FR Higgins, Oliver St John Gogarty, Thomas MacDonagh and Patrick (Pádraig) Pearse.

The founding of the Abbey Theatre was a crowning achievement of the Literary Revival.

The Irish Literary Revival was a cultural movement, but many of the writers involved were also political nationalists, and it is no coincidence that many of the leaders of the Easter Rising of 1916, for example, were poets and writers.

collected folklore from the local people and wrote it down in 'Kiltartanese'.

The famous poet WB Yeats, the leading figure in the Irish Literary Revival, became a great friend of hers. He admired her work as a folklorist and her use of Hiberno-English in her writing. She was a pioneer in this, and writers like JM Synge followed her example.

Yeats spent a lot of time on Lady Gregory's estate at Coole Park, near Gort in County Galway. Later he lived in a nearby castle, Thoor Ballylee. There is a large copper beech tree still standing in the garden at Coole, which is called the Autograph Tree. Yeats and other visiting writers carved their initials into its bark.

As well as writing her own plays, Lady Gregory worked closely with Yeats on his. *Cathleen Ní Houlihan*, which was performed and published under his name, was in fact written jointly. Yeats did not admit this publicly, but he did acknowledge her important role in his life's work in the Irish Literary Revival when he was awarded the Nobel Prize for Literature in 1923.

With their shared interest in Irish literature and drama, WB Yeats and Lady Gregory wanted to have a theatre that would put on plays by Irish dramatists. Together, and with the help of other like-minded people, they founded the Abbey Theatre in Dublin in 1904. This became Ireland's national theatre. It was and still is an extremely important national cultural institution.

Between them, Lady Gregory and WB Yeats ran the Abbey Theatre. They put on plays by JM Synge, George Bernard Shaw and Sean O'Casey as well as by themselves. Lady Gregory's own plays were extremely popular and brought in the crowds to the Abbey. They were mostly well-constructed romantic comedies. Some of them were still being put on as school plays until quite recently.

The Abbey was a nationalist theatre. But not all nationalists saw things the way the Abbey did. In fact there was a riot when they put on Synge's *The Playboy of the Western World* in 1907. The leader of Sinn Féin, Arthur Griffith, said it was 'a vile and inhuman story told in the foulest language we have ever listened to from a public platform'.

Some years later, Lady Gregory took the Abbey production of the *Playboy* to the USA. She was treated as a celebrity, especially by Irish America. She was invited to the White House to meet the president, William Howard Taft. However, there was a riot also in New York when the play was put on there. Potatoes, stink bombs and rosary-beads were thrown onto the stage and the actors were arrested and put on trial.

Lady Gregory's only son, Robert, was killed in action during World War I, fighting 'for king and country'. This was a terrible blow to her and his death inspired Yeats's very fine poem 'An Irish Airman Foresees his Death'.

Although her family, including her son, were unionists, Lady Gregory herself had become more and more nationalist in her outlook over the decades. During the War of Independence (1919–21) Lady Gregory wrote articles for *The Nation* newspaper describing the violent crimes of the Black and Tans (British forces brought in to quash the rebellion). These articles were published anonymously but it was known locally that she had written them. Because of this, Coole was not burnt down by the IRA, which is what happened to most of the big houses of the landlords around that time.

During the Civil War (1922–3) Lady Gregory was threatened by a tenant. In response she told him that she sat at her window every evening with the shutters open, and said he could easily shoot her if he wanted to. He didn't. She lived for another decade and died of an illness at home at Coole.

Writing many years after her death, the critic Mary Colum said that without Lady Gregory a theatre like the Abbey would almost certainly not have been established. 'With all her faults and snobbery, she was a great woman, a real leader ...'

From 'Beautiful Lofty Things'

Augusta Gregory seated at her great ormolu table,
Her eightieth winter approaching:
'Yesterday he threatened my life.
I told him that nightly from six to seven I sat at this table,
The blinds drawn up.'

by WB Yeats

Lady Gregory

Fact File

1852 Born Isabella Augusta Persse in Roxborough House (later burnt down) near Loughrea, County Galway, to an Anglo-Irish landed family.

1880 Married Sir William Henry Gregory, a former MP and governor of Ceylon (now Sri Lanka), who was 35 years older than she was.

1881 Her only child, Robert, was born.

1892 Her husband died.

1896 Met WB Yeats, who was to become an important friend and colleague.

1899 With WB Yeats and Edward Martyn, founded the Irish Literary Theatre, which later led to the foundation of the Abbey Theatre.

1902 Published *Cuchulain of Muirthemne*.

1904 Published *Gods and Fighting Men*.

1904 Co-founded the Abbey Theatre with Yeats and others.

1904 Her play *Spreading the News* was the first to be performed on the Abbey stage; this play was later one of seven by her published as *Seven Short Plays*.

1906–10 Published books of folklore: *A Book of Saints and Wonders*, *The Kiltartan History Book*, *The Kiltartan Wonder Book*.

1911 Took the Abbey production of *The Playboy of the Western World* to America.

1921 Established Irish PEN, an organisation of writers, with links to sister organisations worldwide.

1932 Died at home in Coole.

Constance Markievicz

1868–1927

Countess Markievicz took an active part in the 1916 Rising as a lieutenant in the Irish Citizen Army and was the first woman elected to Westminster

Constance Markievicz came from an Anglo-Irish family, the Gore-Booths of County Sligo. Although her family were landed gentry and a bit eccentric, they were socially minded. Both Constance and her sister Eva were suffragettes and labour activists. Constance founded the Sligo Suffrage Campaign as a young woman. She got the title 'Countess' when she married a Polish count, Casimir Markievicz (though whether or not he really was a count is not clear).

Constance studied art in London. Her parents were dead set against this, but Constance was determined, and in the end she got her way. She came back to Ireland, with her husband, in the early years of the 20th century. They had a daughter, Maeve, who was raised mostly by Constance's mother in Sligo.

Constance and Casimir were leading lights in artistic circles in Dublin. Constance also became active in nationalist politics, trade unionism and the women's suffrage movement.

She was considered to be a noisy, boisterous person, but she had a kind heart. She looked after anyone in need who came to her home, Surrey House in Leinster Road in Rathmines. She put them up and gave them money, keeping little for herself.

She got on well with boys, and she helped set up the Fianna, a nationalist boy-scouting movement. Countess Markievicz took the Fianna boys camping in the Dublin mountains at the weekends. The Fianna were also involved in military training, some of which took place in Surrey House.

Constance Markievicz was a socialist and a strong supporter of trade unions, especially the Irish Women Workers' Union. In 1913, the factory owners of Dublin wanted the workers to give up their trade union membership. When the workers refused, the owners locked the gates of the factories and refused to pay their employees. A man called James Connolly set up a social- ist volunteer force called the Irish Citizen Army in response

From 'In Memory of Eva Gore-Booth and Con Markiewicz'

The light of evening, Lissadell,
Great windows open to the south,
Two girls in silk kimonos, both
Beautiful, one a gazelle.
But a raving autumn shears
Blossom from the summer's wreath;
The older is condemned to death,
Pardoned, drags out lonely years ...

by WB Yeats

Camping with the Fianna

'Tents are very hard to pitch if you don't know how, especially at night. Whenever you trip over a rope in the dark the peg comes out, you probably fall on to the tent, and it collapses. Anyhow the peg flies out and is lost. Next comes the task of trying to disentangle jam from blankets, frying pans, cushions, poetry books and all the other indispensable articles that we had brought. Candles were the only important thing we had forgotten. But at last everything had found a place, the boys were comfortably settled and we turned in and drifted into dreamland.'

Constance Markievicz

to police violence during the Lockout. Constance joined this army. She was also one of the women who set up and ran a soup kitchen in Liberty Hall during the Lockout. (Hanna Sheehy Skeffington, Kathleen Lynn and Dorothy Stopford Price were also involved in the soup kitchen.)

The Irish Citizen Army went on to fight, along with the Irish Volunteers, in the Easter Rising of 1916. Constance was also a member of Cumann na mBan, the women's section of the Irish Volunteers. Members of Cumann na mBan were not expected to fight. But Constance was a lieutenant in the Citizen Army, and she fought in St Stephen's Green and later in the College of Surgeons. There were rumours that she deliberately shot an unarmed policeman. But there is no evidence that this ever happened.

When the rebels surrendered, she was court-martialled and sentenced to death. Because she was a woman, she was not executed. This did not please her – she wanted to die alongside her comrades. Instead she was sent to Aylesbury Prison in England and later released.

When the Great War (now known as World War I) came to an end in 1918, elections were held. For the first time, women were allowed to vote and to stand for election. Countess Markievicz stood for Sinn Féin – even though she was in prison again for republican activities – and won a seat. She was the first woman ever elected to the Westminster parliament. However, Sinn Féin had a policy of not taking their seats. So even though Countess Markievicz was an MP, she never actually sat in the House of Commons.

Sinn Féin candidates who had won seats in the 1918 election assembled in the Mansion House, Dublin, in January 1919. They declared themselves Dáil Éireann. Constance was made Minister for Labour. She had to fight very hard to get Éamon de Valera to give her this recognition.

She was in and out of prison again over the next few years, on various charges. When she was free, she cycled round Dublin in disguise.

During the War of Independence, she helped Michael Collins in a guerrilla campaign. The British finally decided to come to an agreement with the Irish. But there was opposition to the Anglo-Irish Treaty. It did not properly recognise the republic, but made Ireland a 'dominion'. Constance opposed the Treaty in Dáil debates.

The Civil War (between pro- and anti-Treaty people) broke out in 1922. Constance fought on the anti-Treaty side. She was the only woman to carry arms.

After the Civil War came to an end in 1923, Countess Markievicz won a seat in the Dáil. But this was now a post-Treaty Dáil and taking her seat would mean having to swear an oath of allegiance to the king. She refused the oath and did not take her seat. Shortly after that she was imprisoned yet again for making speeches supporting hunger-striking republican prisoners. She went on hunger strike herself, and was later released.

When De Valera founded Fianna Fáil in 1926, Constance was not entirely happy about the new party. She joined all the same. She won a large majority in her last election campaign in 1927. She died shortly afterwards, in poverty, among the poor people she had always worked for.

'My idea is the Workers' Republic for which Connolly died, and a real Treaty between a free Ireland and a free England … I have seen the stars and I am not going to follow a flickering will-o'-the-wisp.'

from a speech to the Dáil by Constance Markievicz in 1922

Countess Markievicz was one of the many women whose activities during the revolutionary years were gradually 'written out of history'. She was mostly remembered as an eccentric figure, not to be taken seriously. She was jeered at for wearing breeches (trousers) during the Easter Rising. She and other women TDs were later blamed for the Civil War, for making over-emotional speeches during Dáil debates and stirring up the men.

People also said that Constance was a neglectful mother. It is true that she did not see much of her daughter, Maeve, who was brought up by Constance's own mother. However, Maeve came to see Constance when she was dying. So did her husband and her stepson; she had always been very fond of him.

> 'During the recent election she broke both bones of her lower arm with the starting handle of her ancient car.
> All she said while they were being set was: "Glory be, it's not my jaw: I can still talk." And with her arm in a sling she went on to her meeting and made her speech.'
>
> *Reginald Roper, writing in* The Nation *on Constance's death*

Countess Markievicz

Fact File

1868 Born Constance Gore-Booth at Lissadell House, County Sligo, the eldest of three girls and two boys.

1892 Went to London to study at the Slade School of Art.

1897 Constance's sister Eva moved to Manchester and became involved in the suffragette movement.

1900 Constance married Casimir Markievicz, whom she had met in Paris.

1901 Her daughter Maeve was born.

1905 Constance and Casimir were among the founders of the United Arts Club in Dublin.

1908 Campaigned with her sister Eva and Eva's friend Esther Roper in a by-election in Manchester, her first experience of electioneering.

1908 Joined Inghinidhe na hÉireann (a revolutionary women's organisation founded by Maud Gonne, later amalgamated with Cumann na mBan).

1909 Joined the council of Sinn Féin – not the party we know by that name today, but a moderate movement founded by Arthur Griffith.

1909 With Bulmer Hobson, founded the Fianna, a boy-scout movement with a military aspect.

1910 The Abbey produced Casimir's play, *The Memory of the Dead*, in which Constance played the lead; it was a great success.

1913 With other women labour activists, set up a soup kitchen in Liberty Hall during the Great Lockout; joined the Irish Citizen Army and became joint treasurer.

Countess Markievicz

Fact File

1913 Constance's husband left Ireland; he fought for Poland in the war and was wounded; they never lived together again, but remained on good terms.

1916 Fought in the Easter Rising, was court-martialled and sentenced to death, but instead was imprisoned.

1917 Received into the Roman Catholic church.

1917 Joined Sinn Féin.

1918 Imprisoned for alleged participation in a 'German plot'; elected to Westminster while still in prison; did not take her seat even when released.

1919 The first Dáil Éireann was set up; Constance managed to get De Valera to make her a minister.

1920 Arrested again for 'conspiracy' and sentenced to two years' hard labour.

1921 Released after the truce with Britain.

1922 Visited America on a trip to raise support for the anti-Treaty side.

1922–3 Fought in the Civil War on the anti-Treaty side.

1923 Imprisoned again for supporting hunger-striking republican prisoners; went on hunger strike herself; later released.

1926 Joined Fianna Fáil.

1926 Her sister Eva died; Constance devastated.

1927 Won another election, but died shortly afterwards.

Peig Sayers

1873–1958

Peig Sayers wrote a famous autobiography that describes a traditional way of life in an Irish-speaking island community from a female perspective

Peig Sayers's autobiography, usually called simply *Peig*, is probably the best-known book in the Irish language. The reason for this is that it was on the secondary school curriculum for decades and was read by most students as part of their studies in Irish. It is an important book, because, unlike most books written in Irish at the time, it gives us insights into what life was like for poor women living in remote Gaeltacht areas a hundred years ago.

Peig was from Dún Chaoin (Dunquin) on the Dingle peninsula in County Kerry. She grew up speaking Irish at home. She was clever and loved school, but she had to leave early because her family was poor. She was sent to work for a family in the nearby town of Dingle. These people were kind to her and encouraged her to keep up her reading.

After two years in Dingle, Peig fell ill and had to go home. When she recovered, she went to work for another family. This was a very different experience. She says in her books that she had to work like a slave.

Peig had a great friend called Cáit Jim. Like many young Irish people, Cáit Jim emigrated to America, and the plan was that when she had saved up enough money, she would send Peig her fare, and Peig would follow her to America. Cáit was not able to send the money, though, so Peig had to stay at home and try to make a life for herself.

When Peig's brother got married, it was clear that Peig was going to have to move out of home. Her brother's wife was the

> *Is ar scáth a chéile a mhaireas na daoine.*
>
> This is probably the best-known sentence from Peig's book. It means: 'The people live in each other's shadow.'
>
> It describes the closeness and neighbourliness of the island people.

Peig

Unfortunately, young people up and down the
country were forced to study *Peig* for their exams,
and that turned many of them against it. *Peig* is an
important document, but it is not really appealing
reading for most young people. Also, the very
rich and beautiful Irish in which it is written was
probably too difficult for a lot of students. The
result is that *Peig*, though very well known, is not
popular. It would be true to say, all the same, that
Peig has acquired mythic status among older people
in Ireland who read her book when they were at
school – even if they did not like it.

Peig's story is sometimes accused of being depressing,
and she certainly had a hard life. But it was a
remarkable achievement, considering her situation, that
a woman like Peig gained the reputation that she did
and became world-renowned as a source of information
and stories about her way of life.

Peig is no longer on school reading lists, and
nowadays it is more likely to be read by adults who
are interested in the Irish language or in Irish social
history – who are the proper audience for it.

> Agus ba ghearr gur aithin a comharsana ansiúd (ar an oileán) gurbh ardseanchaí í seo a bhí tagtha mar dhuine orthu.
>
> It wasn't long before her neighbours there (on the island) recognised that the woman who had come among them was a great storyteller.
>
> *from* Beatha Pheig Sayers, *edited by* Micheál Ó Gaoithín

woman of the house now in the family home. The best thing seemed to be for Peig herself to get married. In those days, it was usual for marriages to be arranged in rural Ireland, and the girl might not always have a lot of say in whom she married.

Peig did not want to marry someone she did not love. Young girls were not supposed to have ideas like this at that time, and indeed Peig kept her thoughts to herself. But in her books, written when she was older, Peig has a lot to say about how difficult marriage could make life for a woman.

Luckily, the match that Peig's father had in mind was very acceptable to her. The man in question was an islandman called Peatsaí Flint Ó Guithín. Peig's family may not have known it, but she had already fallen for this fine young man. She knew that if she married Peatsaí, she would have to live on the Great Blasket island, where life was very tough. But she thought it was better than having to work like a slave, and she would have her own home.

When they married (in 1892), Peig went to live with her husband on the island. Like all the island women, she did not take her husband's surname when she got married. In the 19th century this was very unusual, but it was the local custom.

The island life that Peig describes was very harsh. The people were poor and it was hard to put food on the table, not to mention luxuries. The men fished and farmed. The women helped out on the land, looked after the house and the children, kept the fire in and did the cooking, and they knitted and sewed and sometimes kept hens. Especially in the winter time, the seas could be treacherous and fishermen were often drowned. But, as Peig says, there are two sides to every story. Even though life was difficult, it could also be joyful and the people helped each other out in times of need. Peig and her husband had eleven children, five of whom died as infants or in childhood. All Peig's children emigrated, though one of her sons returned to the island.

Peig herself did not physically write the book we know as *Peig*. She learned to read and write English at school, but she had never learned to write in Irish. Instead, she dictated her story to her son Mícheál (or Maidhc – pronounced Mike – nicknamed 'An File', the poet). He sent the manuscript to a woman called Máire Ní Chinnéide, who had encouraged Peig to write her story.

It seems likely that Peig's story was changed a fair bit before it was published, either by Mícheál or Máire or both of them. Also, Peig herself had probably been careful about what she said in a book that was going to be read by the public. Everyone would have wanted Peig to come across as respectable, because that was important at the time, especially for poorer people.

A few years later, another version of Peig's autobiography was published. Long after Peig's death, Mícheál published yet another biography of his mother. This third book was called *Beatha Pheig Sayers* ('The Life of Peig Sayers'). The Peig we meet in that book is a much more strong-willed and independent-minded woman than the Peig we know from the school textbook. It may be that Mícheál felt he could allow his mother's true voice to be heard now that she was no longer alive.

One reason Peig was asked to write her life story is that she was a gifted storyteller. Her father was a *seanchaí*, and he had passed a lot of his stories to her, along with his gift for storytelling. She also got stories from Nain, the mother of her first employer in Dingle. As well as her autobiographies, Peig also dictated hundreds of traditional tales, anecdotes, ghost stories and proverbs from her rich store of *seanchas*.

People who met Peig and heard her talking were enchanted by her use of language. Scholars and people interested in Irish folklore and the Irish language would visit her from many countries of the world when she was an old woman. She would sit in the best chair by the fire – a seat usually reserved for men – and smoke her pipe and sometimes take a little whiskey, and talk to the professors and folklorists. She had plenty to say for herself. It was some achievement for a poor woman of little formal education to be receiving important international scholars in her humble cottage. Her strength of character, dignity and independence of spirit must have drawn people to her, as well as her great store of *seanchas*.

Nobody has lived on the Great Blasket since 1953. (Peig herself had already left some years before that, and gone back to the mainland.) The fishing community who lived there had to deal with harsh conditions and they were poor. Over the years the population went down, because most of the young people emigrated. (Emigration was very common all over Ireland at the time, especially in poor rural communities.) By the time the island was abandoned in 1953, there were only twenty-two people living on it.

The Great Blasket is a very beautiful place, and it is popular today with tourists. In particular, people like to go there to see the stars in the night sky, unspoilt by street lights, house lights and the lights of cars. If you visit the island today you can stay in Peig's actual house, which has been renovated and turned into a hostel. In Peig's time, it would have been a much simpler and more basic dwelling, and of course there would have been no central heating, electricity, running water, phone or Wi-Fi.

Peig Sayers

Fact File

1873 Born Maighréad Sayers in Vicarstown, Dún Chaoin (Dunquin), County Kerry, the youngest child of an Irish-speaking family; Peig is a common pet name for people called Maighréad or Margaret, and the little girl was known in her family as Peig Bhuí (Yellow Peig) because of her blond hair.

1892 Peig married Peatsaí Flint Ó Guithín and went to live on the Great Blasket island.

1936 *Peig – a Scéal Féin* ('Peig – Her Own Story', usually called simply *Peig*), an autobiography dictated by Peig to her son, was published.

1939 *Machnamh Seanmhná* (*An Old Woman's Reflections*), a second autobiography, also dictated by Peig to her son, was published.

1942 Peig, who was now a widow, left the island and went back to Dún Chaoin on the mainland, where she was from.

1953 The Great Blasket island was abandoned; it is still uninhabited today, but it is a popular place for tourists in the summer time.

1958 Death of Peig Sayers in the hospital in Dún Chaoin on the Dingle peninsula.

1962 *Peig* was put on the school curriculum and was studied by students all over Ireland for their leaving certificate examination.

1970 A third biography of Peig, *Beatha Pheig Sayers* ('The Life of Peig Sayers'), written by her son, was published; it gives different versions of many incidents told in Peig's other two autobiographies – we are probably getting to know the real Peig in this later autobiography, published long after her death.

1974 An English translation of *Peig* was published.

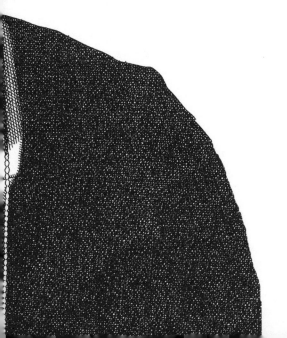

Hanna Sheehy Skeffington

1877–1946

Hanna Sheehy Skeffington was a leading campaigner for women's rights and a republican

Hanna Sheehy Skeffington is best known as an activist for women's suffrage – women's right to vote. She was involved in this struggle for many years and was in and out of prison for her activities. She was also a republican. She wanted Ireland to be independent, but she also wanted Ireland to be a country where men and women had equal rights.

Hanna Sheehy belonged to a political family. Her father was an MP for the Irish Parliamentary Party in the Westminster parliament. One of Hanna's first memories was of visiting her uncle, Fr Eugene Sheehy, known as 'the Land League priest', in Kilmainham Gaol, when she was only 'a chit of four'.

Hanna's parents believed in educating their daughters as well as their sons. Hanna went to the Dominican convent school on Eccles Street in Dublin. She was a model student and won prizes that helped to pay for her education.

Even though women sat the same university examinations as the male students, they had no access to the university libraries, sports facilities or dining halls. Their social lives were also very restricted, and they were not even allowed attend the debating society. Perhaps it was her own experience of this unfairness that led to Hanna becoming seriously interested in equal rights for women.

She wanted to go to university, but at the time Irish universities did not accept women students. However, women could sit university exams and be awarded degrees. Several girls' schools set up university classes, and then developed colleges. Hanna attended St Mary's University College, run by the Dominican nuns, and she went on to get a BA and later an MA from the Royal University of Ireland.

Fr Eugene Sheehy

Hanna's uncle Fr Eugene Sheehy was active with Charles Stewart Parnell and Michael Davitt in the Land League, and was imprisoned along with them for agitating on behalf of tenants. He also supported the Ladies' Land League and was in favour of women taking part in political affairs.

He encouraged Hanna in her studies. He gave her a small antique desk. It was decorated with mother-of-pearl inlay and had all sorts of hidden compartments and drawers. After one of her exam successes, he took her on a trip to London. They went to see where her father worked in the House of Commons.

Years later, he was in the GPO in 1916, tending to the spiritual needs of the rebels.

While a student, Hanna met Francis (Frank) Skeffington. He was an unconventional man who wore tweed knickerbockers and a 'Votes for Women' badge. He was very active in student politics and the debating society, and he was a firm believer in equal rights for women. He and Hanna were married in 1903. Unusually for that time, they decided to combine their surnames as they thought that was more equal than the woman taking the man's surname, so they became the Sheehy Skeffingtons.

> Later in life Hanna recalled that women speakers had to be 'capable of keeping their temper under bombardments of rotten eggs, over-ripe tomatoes, bags of flour and stinking chemicals'.

Shortly after their marriage, Frank campaigned for women to be admitted to University College Dublin on the same basis as men. When the president of the university reprimanded him for this, Frank resigned from his job there as registrar. From then on, Frank worked as a freelance journalist, and Hanna became the main breadwinner. She was a teacher.

Influenced by the English suffragettes Emmeline Pankhurst and her daughters Christabel and Sylvia, Hanna became very interested in the cause of women's suffrage – women's right to vote. She began writing articles and speaking at public meetings. In 1908 she and Frank, together with Margaret and James Cousins, founded the Irish Women's Franchise League (IWFL). They also launched a weekly feminist newspaper, *The Irish Citizen*. Many people were hostile to the idea of women getting the right to vote, but the IWFL had many supporters.

> 'Until the women of Ireland are free, the men will not achieve emancipation.'
>
> *Hanna Sheehy Skeffington*

When the Irish Parliamentary Party (also called the Home Rule Party) refused to support votes for Irish women, Hanna and five other women took militant action. They broke windows at Ship Street Barracks. They were arrested and imprisoned in Mountjoy Prison. While in prison, the women went on hunger strike in protest at how two suffragettes in England were being treated. Hanna was released from prison after her fifth day on hunger strike. She lost her job as a teacher because of this episode.

Hanna was also a founding member of the Irish Women Workers' Union. Both Frank and Hanna supported James Connolly during the Great Lockout of 1913 – when factory owners in Dublin locked all workers who would not give up their union membership out of their places of work, so they could not earn a living. Hanna worked in a soup kitchen, serving food to the families of the locked-out workers. At a demonstration, Hanna was arrested for assaulting a policeman and was imprisoned again.

Hanna did not join Cumann na mBan (the women's section of the republican movement). She did not like the way the Volunteers (all men) were in charge of that organisation. However, she did bring food and messages to the rebels in the GPO during the 1916 Rising. Frank, who was a pacifist, tried to prevent looting in the city during the fighting. An army patrol arrested him along with a couple of newspaper editors, and they were shot dead without trial by an army firing party.

The army tried to cover this up and persuade Hanna to accept compensation for Frank's murder, but she was having none of it. She insisted on a government inquiry into his death, and Frank was shown to be innocent. The man who killed him was court-martialled. But he was declared insane and was released after eighteen months.

Hanna went on a lecture tour of America, talking at more than 250 venues, to raise awareness of Frank's murder, to

Micheline Sheehy Skeffington

Hanna's son Owen grew up to be a lecturer in French at Trinity College Dublin, and he married a Frenchwoman. They were both involved in the labour movement, and Owen's wife Andrée became known for her work for women's causes.

In 2014, their daughter Micheline won an important Equality Tribunal case against NUI Galway. She claimed she was discriminated against by the university, which did not promote her because of her gender. The tribunal took into account the record of the university in promoting men and women. Over a period of eight years, 50 men were promoted to the position of senior lecturer, compared with only 11 women.

'Men don't get it,' Dr Sheehy Skeffington said. 'Women know exactly what this case is about.' A major reason that she took the case was to honour her grandmother's achievements on women's behalf. 'I have it in the genes. If I see an injustice I have to do something about it.'

In 2017, Micheline Sheehy Skeffington undertook a trip to America by boat, following in her grandmother's footsteps and speaking at some of the same venues a hundred years later.

> 'Under the 1916 Proclamation Irish women were given equal citizenship, equal rights and equal opportunities, and subsequent constitutions have filched these or smothered them in mere "empty formulae".'
>
> *Hanna Sheehy Skeffington*

speak out about the war and against British rule in Ireland, and to raise funds for Sinn Féin. Because she had been refused a passport, she and her young son, Owen, travelled under the names of Mrs Gribben and her son Eugene. When she returned to Ireland in July 1917, Hanna disguised herself as a workman while travelling in the hold of a boat. She was arrested shortly after arriving in Dublin and was sent to Holloway Prison in England, but was released a few days after she went on hunger strike.

Hanna Sheehy Skeffington and other women who shared her views did eventually succeed in getting the vote for women, in both Britain and Ireland, in 1918. Hanna continued to be politically active. She had joined Sinn Féin in 1917, and during the War of Independence she was a judge in the republican courts (set up as an alternative to the official courts). She was a member of the Fianna Fáil party for a short period.

She founded the Women's Prisoners Defence League along with Maud Gonne and Charlotte Despard in 1922 to support republican prisoners. In 1933, she went to Northern Ireland to speak on behalf of the female republican prisoners in Armagh Gaol. She had been barred from Northern Ireland and was arrested yet again.

When the Irish constitution was being drawn up, she opposed the articles in it that refer to women's role in the home. Some years later she founded a women's political party, the Women's

Social and Political League. She stood for election for that party, but did not win a seat.

Hanna Sheehy Skeffington was born in the 19th century, but she is very much a woman of our time. She fought for women's rights and spoke out against discrimination and unfairness – things women are still having to fight today.

Women and the Constitution

Irish women are still protesting against the articles in the constitution that Hanna objected to back in 1937:

Article 42.2.1
In particular, the State recognises that by her life within the home, woman gives to the State a support without which the common good cannot be achieved.

Article 41.2.2
The State shall, therefore, endeavour to ensure that mothers shall not be obliged by economic necessity to engage in labour to the neglect of their duties in the home.

Hanna Sheehy Skeffington

Fact File

1877 Born Johanna Sheehy in Kanturk, County Cork, the eldest of a family of six – she had three sisters and two brothers; her father was a Member of Parliament and her uncle was a Land League activist.

1899 Got a BA degree in modern languages (French and German).

1902 After spending some time in Paris and in Bonn, Hanna came back to Dublin and got an MA degree with first class honours.

1903 Married fellow student and feminist Francis Skeffington.

1908 Hanna and Francis founded the Irish Women's Franchise League (IWLF) with Margaret and James Cousins; Hanna arrested when she broke windows as part of a protest.

1909 Hanna and Frank's only child, Owen, was born.

1913 Hanna and Frank supported the labour movement during the Lockout.

1916 Frank shot dead by the British army.

1917 Hanna joined Sinn Féin.

1917 Went on a lecture tour of America to highlight what had

Hanna Sheehy Skeffington

Fact File

happened to Frank and to raise
money for the republican cause.

1920 Elected to Dublin
Corporation.

1922 Was co-founder of the
Women's Prisoners Defence
League.

1922 Sent to America by
Éamon de Valera to raise money
for the republican cause.

1926 Joined Fianna Fáil but left
soon afterwards.

1933 Arrested for entering
Northern Ireland to speak out
in support of women republican
prisoners.

1935 Opposed the Conditions
of Employment Bill.

1937 Campaigned against the
articles concerning women in
the Irish constitution.

1937 Helped found the
Women's Social and Political
League (WSPL).

1943 Stood for election along
with three other independent
women candidates endorsed by
the WSPL in a general election;
all of them were defeated.

1946 Died.

Eileen Gray

1878–1976

Eileen Gray was one of the greatest designers of the 20th century with a huge international reputation

In 2009, an armchair designed by Eileen Gray was sold at auction in Paris for almost €22 million – which the purchaser called 'the price of desire'. This is by far the most money ever paid for a piece of 20th-century design. It shows what an amazing reputation Eileen Gray had more than thirty years after her death. She is without doubt our most famous designer.

Eileen Gray lived most of her adult life in Paris, with time spent also in other parts of France and in London, but she was always very proud to be Irish. Born in County Wexford, Eileen spent much of her childhood in Ireland. Like most girls from well-off families at the time, she was educated at home. She enjoyed boating on the River Slaney and going to the Dublin Horse Show in the summer. Her father was a painter, and he often took her on his painting trips to Europe.

> 'It was a happy childhood that seemed like one long sunny summer ... days and days of being with the horses and down by the river and picking great branches of flowering bushes for the house.'
>
> *Eileen Gray*

Eileen inherited her father's artistic talent. She studied at the Slade School of Art in London and later in Paris. She was a fine painter and she painted throughout her life, moving from figurative to abstract styles. She liked playing with geometric shapes and with swirling or straight lines. She designed carpets and rugs and brought her sense of shape and colour from her experience as a painter into her carpet designs. She was also a superb photographer, a sculptor and an architect, but she is probably best known for her furniture designs.

In the early 20th century, Paris was buzzing with new ideas and developments in art. It was the perfect place for Eileen Gray, who was always open to new ideas and movements in art. She was interested in the work of artists such as Whistler, Aubrey Beardsley, Picasso, Braque; the ballets of Diaghilev; the poetry of Apollinaire. She took a particular interest in developments in Cubism and other movements in abstract art. She was friendly in Paris with the Irish artist Mainie Jellett, who later became a champion of Cubism in Ireland. Mainie Jellett also designed carpets and her designs were influenced by Eileen Gray.

While she was studying art at the Slade, Eileen became interested in the traditional Japanese art of lacquering, and she continued working with lacquer when she moved to Paris. Lacquer is a very hard, glossy finish that is applied to the surface of furniture – like a decorative varnish. Because the lacquer has to be applied in a very humid environment, Eileen used to do it in her bathroom, until she got a studio. She was always experimenting with different colours, adding natural pigments to the lacquer. She was the first person to succeed in creating a blue lacquer, using her own secret recipe.

She started by making small lacquer pieces, and went on to make large and beautiful lacquer screens and panels for which she became famous. At the same time, she was also designing furniture – chairs, tables, beds, dressing tables.

With an American friend, she opened a carpet workshop, where a team of women produced carpets using her designs for several years. Some of the carpets had Irish themes and had titles like 'Kilkenny', 'Wexford', 'Irish Green'. Some of Eileen Gray's carpet designs were used by Donegal Carpets in the 1970s.

Over time, Eileen Gray became interested in different finishes for her furniture. She pioneered the use of new materials and surfaces like chrome and tubular steel. In the 1920s she started to design radically new pieces of furniture, very modern and innovative. Around this time, she opened an interiors shop in Paris, called Jean Désert. It was described in the *Chicago Tribune* as an 'adventure: an experience with the unheard of,

The lacquering process

Making lacquer is very slow and painstaking – the whole process can take up to nine months!

1. First, cut into bark of a Rhus tree and collect the sap (which is very toxic) in seashells.
2. Stir repeatedly in mixing bowl for eight days.
3. Filter out impurities; it looks like melted chocolate, a dense liquid which dries slowly to form a hard surface.
4. Pigments can be added in, or it can be left in its natural colour.
5. Paint the lacquer onto wood which is primed by covering it with silk gauze applied with rice gum. Use a paintbrush made from Chinese men's hair. (The hair runs the length of the brush, which is sharpened like a pencil.)
6. Each layer is painted in a very humid environment. Each piece has twenty to thirty layers of lacquer, with each coat taking up to ten days to dry.
7. When dry, the lacquer is rubbed with charcoal, then polished – first with oil, then with a mixture of oil and a Japanese clay called Tomoko, and finally with gazelle-horn powder.

Note: the lacquering process is dangerous to health. Eileen suffered quite bad skin reactions. Don't try this in your own bathroom!

a sojourn into the never-before-seen'. It attracted collectors, artists and socialites, and it gained an international reputation.

The shop closed in 1930, but Eileen continued to design and produce furniture. She was often commissioned to design not just individual pieces of furniture, but to fit out whole apartments. She would design the curtains, rugs to hang on the walls and screens and panels, as well as the furniture and the light fittings.

From an early age Eileen was interested in architecture. At that time, it was almost impossible for a woman to become an architect. But although she had no formal training in architecture, she went on to design a house in the south of France, which was named 'E.1027', for her partner Jean Badovici. Badovici was himself an architect. He encouraged Eileeen's architectural ambitions and they worked on many projects together. The plan was for the couple to live in this house, but they broke up soon afterwards. (They remained lifelong friends, however.)

E.1027 was built on a steep hillside overlooking the Bay of Monaco, with fantastic views. Eileen designed everything to do with the house – fittings, furniture, décor, as well as the building itself. The most famous architect in France at the time was Le Corbusier. He believed that a house is a 'machine for living in'. Eileen Gray had a different idea. 'A house is not a machine for living in,' she said. 'It is the shell of man. His extension, his release, his spiritual emanation ...'

> The house Eileen Gray designed for Jean Badovici was called E.1027:
>
> E = Eileen
> 10 = J, first letter of Jean
> 2 = B, first letter of Badovici
> 7 = G, first letter of Gray

In designing her stunning house, she thought all the time of how best it could be lived in at different times of the day and in different social situations. She aimed for 'minimum of space,

Famous Eileen Gray designs

- Adjustable table – a lightweight multi-purpose table whose height can be adjusted; probably her most famous piece of furniture
- 'Architectural cabinet', which could expand sideways to hold large drawings and plans
- 'Bibendum chair' (based on the 'Michelin Man', whose body was made up of stacked tyres), which has a stacked cylindrical backrest
- E.1027 house
- 'Magician of the Night' and 'Milky Way' lacquer screens
- 'Non conformist armchair', with only one arm – Gray had noticed that most people tend to sit slightly to the side
- 'Pirogue' – a canoe-shaped sofabed
- 'Rocket lamp', whose lacquered base resembles a rocket, with a parchment lampshade (some of her lamp designs also included ostrich eggs)
- 'Transat' (= *Transatlantique*) chair, inspired by folding deck chairs

maximum of comfort'. She paid great attention to detail. The rooms had lots of built-in cabinets and drawers, nooks to sit in quietly, little windows with amazing views, and specially designed furniture that could be opened up and extended and folded down again after use. These were all astonishing new ideas at that time.

E.1027 is now considered to be one of the great masterpieces of 20th-century architecture worldwide – and it was designed by an Irishwoman with no formal training in architecture. It is open to the public.

Eileen Gray was very interested in town planning and in trying to find ways to build affordable housing as well as creating spaces for recreation and to meet the needs of children. She designed very imaginative social housing which she hoped could be prefabricated and mass produced. But unfortunately, most of her architectural projects were never built.

Eileen stayed in France during World War II, but was forced to move more than once. She had other homes in France, which were damaged in the war. She disappeared from public view from the 1930s onwards, but she continued to work throughout her long life, painting and designing. She was always exploring new ideas and new materials.

An article in an important architectural magazine in 1968 brought her work back to people's notice. Exhibitions of her designs for buildings, interiors and other projects were held in London, Dublin, Paris, Los Angeles and Vienna. A London-based furniture company started to make furniture using some of her designs.

In 2000 the National Museum of Ireland bought Gray's personal collection from her apartment in Paris, including furniture, models and personal effects. There is a permanent Eileen Gray exhibition in Collins Barracks (part of the National Museum in Dublin). She became the first woman to be commemorated on an Irish coin – on a special limited-edition €10 coin.

Eileen Gray

Fact File

1878 Born Eileen Smith at Brownswood House, Enniscorthy, County Wexford, the daughter of an aristocratic mother and a middle-class father.

1895 Her mother inherited the title Baroness Gray and the family name was changed to Gray – Eileen's parents had separated by then.

1900 Enrolled at the Slade School of Art in London.

1902 Settled in Paris and became part of a wide artistic and cultural circle – painters, sculptors, writers, philosophers.

1910 Started making lacquer-work screens.

1918 Commissioned to design the interior of an apartment by a wealthy society hostess, her first major commission.

c. **1920** Met and fell in love with Jean Badovici, a Romanian architect, for whom she would design a house that became her most famous creation.

Eileen Gray

Fact File

1922 Opened an interiors shop in Paris, Jean Désert.

1926–9 Eileen Gray's famous house E.1027 was designed and built.

1929 Eileen's family home in County Wexford, Brownswood, was sold to the Wexford Health Board and turned into a sanatorium; nowadays it houses a secondary school, Meánscoil Gharmáin.

1930 Jean Désert closed.

1931 Commissioned to design several pieces for the Maharaja of Indore, who was building a modern palace in India.

1968 Article in an architectural journal revived interest in Eileen Gray, who had been largely forgotten since the 1930s.

1976 Died in Paris after a fall in her apartment on her way to her workroom at the age of 98.

2000 National Museum of Ireland bought the contents of her Paris apartment.

2010 Commemorative €10 coin struck.

Dorothy Stopford Price

1890–1954

Dr Dorothy Stopford Price was a leading expert in childhood TB and was key to eradicating TB in Ireland

There was a serious epidemic of tuberculosis (TB) in Ireland in the first half of the 20th century. This dangerous disease was only eradicated (or very nearly eradicated) when a vaccine called BCG started to be widely used. Dorothy Stopford Price was the key figure in bringing the BCG vaccine to Ireland and campaigning for its widespread use. She helped to save thousands of lives.

Dorothy Stopford was born in Dublin to well-to-do Protestant parents. Her grandfather on one side was a doctor (Master of the Rotunda Hospital); her other grandfather was a clergyman and her great-grandfather a bishop. When Queen Victoria died, Dorothy had to wear black for mourning.

Shortly after that, when she was about 12, her father died of typhoid fever. The family moved to England, and Dorothy went to school in London. She came back to Dublin as a young woman to study medicine at Trinity College, which was by then accepting women students.

Dorothy had only just arrived back in Dublin from England when the 1916 Rising broke out. (This was some months before she started at Trinity.) She happened to be a guest of the Under-Secretary for Ireland, Sir Mattew Nathan, in his house in the Phoenix Park when the Rising took place. Sir Matthew was in charge of the country, as his boss, the Chief Secretary, was in London. Dorothy kept a diary at the time, and from this we know that she could hear gunfire from her bedroom in Sir Matthew's house (which is now Áras an Uachtaráin).

Dorothy's aunt Alice Stopford Green was very interested in Irish history and culture and was an active republican. She had been involved with Roger Casement and Erskine Childers in buying and illegally importing arms for the Irish Volunteers in 1914 (an event known as the Howth gun-running). These guns were later used in the Easter Rising of 1916. Dorothy herself was not particularly supportive of the Rising, but like many

Women and university

In the late 19th century, it became possible for women to get university degrees – even though they were not actually able to go to university. Secondary schools – such as Alexandra College and Loreto College Stephen's Green in Dublin, along with many others in the city and around the country – provided university-level tuition to young women, and they were then able to take the university exams and get their degrees.

In 1904, Trinity College Dublin admitted women students for the first time. However, they were only just tolerated. They had to be out of the college by six o'clock every evening, and they certainly could not live in. The college put on separate dissections especially for female medical students, as women were not allowed to attend dissections along with the men.

Even though women could qualify as doctors, there were only about 40 female doctors out of 3000 overall in Ireland in 1916. By the mid-1920s, there were six female doctors in St Ultan's Hospital (founded and run by women), which was more than in all the other Dublin hospitals put together. It was a long time before women were truly able to compete on equal terms with men in the medical field.

> Well over 4000 people were recorded as having died of TB in Ireland in 1922, of whom over 600 were children – but in reality there were probably far more than that. Because it was associated with poverty, people were often ashamed to admit they had TB in the family. That is why it is likely that the figures we have are an under-estimation.

others she became sympathetic to the republican cause when the leaders of the Rising were executed. By the time of the War of Independence (1919–21), Dorothy was a fully fledged republican with links to the Irish Volunteers (old IRA).

She went to work in Kilbrittain dispensary in West Cork as a medical student and stayed on for some time after she qualified as a doctor. The authorities were suspicious of her and they refused her a permit for a bicycle. So the Volunteers supplied her with a pony. She gave talks to the local Volunteers and Cumann na mBan (the women's equivalent of the Irish Volunteers) on how to look after gunshot wounds and stop the bleeding.

At that time (the 1920s), TB was rampant in Dublin. There were no antibiotics that worked against it. The main treatment was sunlight. Hospitals had special wings with terraces built to catch the sun. TB patients would move their chairs around, following the sun throughout the day.

Anyone can get TB, but poor people who live in cramped and damp conditions are more likely to get it. Dorothy Stopford came back to Dublin in 1923 and went to work in St Ultan's Hospital for Infants. The patients in this hospital were poor children from the Dublin slums. Dorothy was horrified at how many of the children had TB. She was desperate to do something about it.

Kathleen Lynn

Like Dorothy Stopford, Kathleen Lynn (1874–1955) also came from a Protestant clerical family. She grew up in Mayo, where she saw terrible poverty and disease. This inspired her to want to become a doctor. She studied in Alexandra College (as the universities were not yet admitting women students) and qualified as a doctor in 1899. When Dr Lynn came back to Dublin after several years in the United States, she became involved in the campaign for women's suffrage (votes for women).

When the Great Lockout happened in 1913, she worked with Countess Markievicz and James Connolly on the side of the workers. She joined Connolly's organisation, the Irish Citizen Army, and was its chief medical officer during the 1916 Rising. She was in City Hall on Easter Monday 1916, and was arrested and imprisoned for some months in Kilmainham Gaol. She remained active in Sinn Féin after the Rising.

She was a committed member of the Church of Ireland, and wanted to Gaelicise that church through Cumann Gaelach hEaglaise na hÉireann.

In 1919, she founded St Ultan's Hospital for Infants, together with her great friend Madeleine ffrench-Mullen, who lived with her. They were supported in this venture by a group of female members of Sinn Féin. The hospital was entirely staffed and run by women. The male medical establishment was not much interested in children's illnesses. Paediatrics – the branch of medicine that is concerned with treating children – was left to women. (It was not even on the syllabus for medical students until 1956.)

Women doctors found it difficult to get employment in hospitals at that time, but there was plenty of work for them in caring for poor women and children, who suffered from illnesses associated with overcrowding and poverty.

Scientists all over Europe were trying to find ways to fight TB. There was a skin test (which used a substance called tuberculin) that made it easier to diagnose TB. This test was viewed with suspicion in Britain and Ireland. On a trip to Vienna, Dorothy found that this skin test was very effective. The trouble was that this test was mostly used in Germany and Austria, and English-speaking doctors did not know much about it. Dorothy learned German and studied in Germany, and she introduced the tuberculin skin test to Ireland.

Meanwhile, two French scientists had invented a vaccine against tuberculosis called BCG. This vaccine was quite effective but it was very controversial at first. It was blamed (possibly incorrectly) for the deaths of seventy-seven children in Germany in 1929–30.

As time went by, BCG was starting to be used more widely in Europe. Dorothy visited hospitals and laboratories in Scandinavia in 1936 and saw BCG being manufactured and used. When she came home, she took out a research licence to use the vaccine in Ireland. She gave

Just around that time, there was a vaccination programme against a different disease, diphtheria, in Ring, County Waterford. Unfortunately, there was some problem (nobody ever found out exactly what it was), and several children got TB as a result of being vaccinated against diphtheria. One young girl died. The 'Ring disaster' had nothing to do with the BCG vaccine, but it made people nervous about vaccination. This meant that Dorothy faced a lot of opposition to her campaign for vaccination with BCG.

the vaccine to thirty-five children in St Ultan's – having got the permission of their parents. This was the first time BCG had been used anywhere in Ireland or Britain, and it was years before it came to be widely used in this country.

When World War II broke out, it became impossible to import BCG from Sweden. After the war, Dorothy started to import it again.

In 1948, Dr Noël Browne, Minister for Health, made Dorothy chairman of a national consultative council on TB. There was some controversy about introducing vaccination nationally, but by 1949 Dorothy was in charge of a mass vaccination programme for the whole population. Dr Pearl Dunlevy, who was on the BCG committee with Dorothy in St Ultan's, had also been active in introducing BCG vaccination into Dublin hospitals. Now at last the vaccination was going to be made available nationally.

Unfortunately, Dorothy became ill soon after that, and was not able to see this work through. She died in 1954. Vaccination with BCG came in as standard practice in the 1950s and TB was vastly reduced. It continued to be given routinely to all babies for decades.

Dorothy Stopford Price

Fact File

1890 Born Dorothy Stopford in Clonskeagh, Dublin, into a middle-class Protestant family.

1902 Her father died and her mother took the family to live in England.

1916 Came back to Ireland from London and was staying in the Phoenix Park when the Easter Rising broke out.

1916 Started to study medicine in Trinity College Dublin.

1921 Graduated with an MB (Bachelor of Medicine) from Trinity, and continued working in Kilbrittain, West Cork, where she had also spent time as a medical student.

1923 Left Kilbrittain and came back to Dublin to work in St Ultan's Hospital for Infants, where she was particularly involved in combating childhood tuberculosis (TB).

1925 Married a barrister called Liam Price; they had no children.

1932 Started to work also as a children's specialist in the Royal City Hospital, Dublin.

Dorothy Stopford Price

Fact File

1935 Received a higher medical degree (MD); her MD thesis was on 'The diagnosis of primary tuberculosis of the lungs in childhood'.

1937 The BCG vaccine arrived in St Ultan's Hospital from Sweden and Dorothy started to use it.

1942 Published *Tuberculosis in Childhood*.

DOROTHY Stopford Price became an internationally recognised expert on TB in children; in addition to her thesis and her book, she wrote many articles in important medical journals.

1949–50 Chaired the National BCG Committee, charged with introducing a national programme of vaccination with BCG.

1954 Died after a long illness.

Mainie Jellett

1897–1944

Mainie Jellett
was an important
20th-century
painter, a pioneer
of Modernism and
abstract art

Art was considered a suitable subject for young ladies when Mainie Jellett started her studies in the Dublin Metropolitan School of Art in 1914. Studying art was not quite as ladylike as people may have thought, though. The famous painter William Orpen daringly allowed his students not only to talk but even to smoke in class. And when he could not find any Irish girls to pose for his life classes – in other words, drawing and painting nudes – he brought models in from London for his students.

Mr Orpen's importation of life models might have shocked some Dubliners, but Mainie Jellett certainly had no problem with learning to draw and paint the human body. Her very beautiful *Bathers*, which she painted some years later after further studies in London, may well have had its beginnings in William Orpen's life classes in Dublin.

Mainie had been painting since she was a child. She came from a well-to-do family and grew up in an elegant house on Fitzwilliam Square in Dublin. Instead of going to school, she was taught at home by governesses and tutors. As young as the age of eleven she was having watercolour lessons from women artists of the day, including WB Yeats's two sisters, Susan and Lily. At only fourteen she went to France, where *plein air* (open-air) landscape painting was all the rage at the time.

Young women who studied art were not really expected to go on to become professional painters in those days. That was for men. Mainie Jellett was passionate about painting, though, and after three years in Dublin she went to London to continue her studies. She was taught by another famous painter, Walter Sickert, at Westminster Art School. She did more life classes there and also learnt more about painting landscapes in both oil and watercolour paints.

Around this time, a new, Modernist way of painting, called Cubism, was being developed in Europe. Mainie Jellett had made friends in London with another Irish artist, Evie Hone.

Cubism

Cubism began in the early 20th century. The famous artist Pablo Picasso was one of the first artists to paint in this new way.

Cubism is an abstract style of painting. Cubist paintings use two-dimensional geometric shapes to create a three-dimensional effect. When you look at a Cubist painting, it is as if you are seeing a 3D object that has been broken and laid flat. The idea is to show things from many different points of view at once.

Cubism is often considered the most important development in art in the 20th century.

Evie Hone

Evie (Eva Sydney) Hone was born to a wealthy Dublin family on 22 April 1894. Her mother died when she was two days old. When Evie was twelve she got polio, which left her frail for the rest of her life. She studied art in London, where she met her lifelong friend, Mainie Jellett.

Deeply religious, Evie entered an Anglican convent in Cornwall in the 1920s. However, she found that the lives of a nun and a painter were not compatible, so she left the convent and chose instead to live her spiritual life through art. She converted to Roman Catholicism in 1937.

Evie Hone was a painter in the Cubist style but she is also well known for her stained glass art. She joined the glass studio An Túr Gloine in Dublin in the 1930s, and later set up her own glass studio.

One of her most famous works in glass, *My Four Green Fields*, depicting the four provinces of Ireland, was commissioned by the Irish government for the Irish pavilion at the 1939 World Fair in New York. It is now in Government Buildings in Dublin.

You can see her windows in churches all over Ireland, for example in St Brendan's Cathedral in Loughrea, County Galway, which also has windows by other An Túr Gloine artists; Church of St John the Baptist in Blackrock, County Dublin; Church of the Holy Family in Ardara, County Donegal.

Evie Hone died suddenly in 1955.

Both Mainie and Evie were interested in Cubism, and together they went to Paris to learn how to paint in this new style. They studied first with André Lhote and later with Albert Gleizes, who were recognised masters of the Cubist style. The two Irishwomen learned much from them about this exciting new way of seeing the world and depicting it in paint.

Not everyone was enthusiastic about the new style of painting, though. When Mainie exhibited her work for the first time in Dublin, in 1923, people scoffed at it and called it 'unfeminine'.

Her painting *Decoration* (painted in 1923) was one of the works in this exhibition. Mainie Jellett was a committed Christian, and this painting in tempera (a kind of paint) and gold leaf on board (instead of canvas) was partly inspired by the 15th-century religious artist Fra Angelico. Most people did not see this connection to medieval religious art. All they saw was that this was abstract art. And they did not like it.

Mainie Jellett realised that the reason people did not appreciate her work was that they did not understand new movements in art. So she began to give public lectures and talks on the radio. She published articles promoting art and explaining Modernism. She taught at the Dublin Metropolitan School of Art. She continued to visit Paris with Evie Hone to keep up their art studies.

As time went by, Mainie became fascinated by the Irish landscape. The Cubist forms in her painting were softened, as can be seen in her picture *Achill Horses* (painted in 1938). In this painting, which uses colours typical of the west of Ireland, the horses seem to become one with the waves of the sea.

Mainie Jellett believed in the spiritual value of colour and she was interested also in Celtic art. As an Anglican (member of the Church of Ireland) from a privileged unionist background, she sometimes felt an outsider in the newly independent Ireland. She went out of her way to try to find ways to communicate with the Catholic majority. In her painting *Virgin of Éire* (painted in 1943), she combines Cubist techniques with vivid colour to create a stunning religious painting.

In 1943 Mainie Jellet was a leader in organising the first Irish Exhibition of Living Art. This was an exhibition of more *avant-garde* (progressive and modern) painting, in contrast to the more old-fashioned art shown at the Royal Hibernian Academy at the time. Sadly, she was unable to attend the exhibition as she developed cancer of the pancreas. She was only forty-six when she died the following year.

Along with other women painters of the time – Mary Swanzy, Norah McGuinness and her great friend Evie Hone – Mainie Jellett made a valuable contribution to the development of Irish art. She also played an important role in educating the public about modern developments in art and helped to change attitudes to abstract art. Even today, however, her work is not always as highly valued as that of male painters.

You can see some of Jellett's paintings, and the work of other Irish women painters of the time, at the National Gallery of Ireland in Dublin (admission free); there are also images online of all the paintings mentioned here.

Mainie Jellett

Fact File

1897 Born Mary Harriet Jellett on 20 April at 36 Fitzwilliam Square, Dublin, her family home; she was the eldest of four girls; her parents were William Morgan Jellett, who was a leading barrister and a Unionist MP, and Janet McKensie Stokes Jellett.

1914 Started her studies at the Dublin Metropolitan School of Art.

1917 Entered the Westminster Art School in London, where she met her lifelong friend Evie Hone.

1921 Went to Paris, where she studied with André Lhote and Albert Gleizes.

1921 Painted *Bathers*, a glorious picture of three female nudes that is both traditional and clearly influenced by Cubist techniques.

1923 Painted *Decoration*, influenced by Cubism but also by early religious art; exhibited at the Dublin Society of Painters.

1928 Painted *Homage to Fra Angelico*, her first painting to be well-reviewed in Ireland.

1932 Won the silver gilt medal for Decorative Painting at the 1932 Aonach Tailteann; also lectured at the Dublin Metropolitan School of Art.

1938 Represented Ireland at the Glasgow Empire Exhibition; painted *Achill Horses*.

1939 Represented Ireland at the World Fair in New York.

1943 Led the organisation of the first Irish Exhibition of Living Art; painted *Virgin of Éire*.

1944 Died in Dublin on 16 February in a nursing home on Leeson Street, Dublin, run by the Sisters of Charity.

1970 Her painting *Virgin of Éire* (painted in 1943) used on an Irish stamp.

Dervla Murphy

born 1931

Dervla Murphy is a
writer who has travelled
the world, often going
to remote places alone,
usually on a bicycle

Dervla Murphy is an unconventional woman who has had a very unusual life. She is well known as a travel writer, but whereas other people travel by plane with family or friends and stay in hotels or campsites, Dervla Murphy usually cycles over vast distances. Until her daughter was born, she always travelled alone. She goes way off the beaten track and meets people who live in remote and non-touristy places.

Even when she is at home, Dervla's way of life is out of the ordinary. She lives in Lismore, County Waterford, which has been her home all her life. She gets up at five o'clock in the morning and eats her breakfast-and-dinner then, and doesn't eat again until the next morning.

'I remember the perfection of my happiness – a perfection not often attained in this life, as I realised even then – when I woke on a dark winter's morning and switched on the light to see a tower of unread library books by my bed ... I could never decide which was the greater pleasure, rereading old favourites or discovering new ones.'

Dervla Murphy

She was an only child. Both of her parents were originally from Dublin, and they moved to Lismore when her father got work there as a county librarian, before Dervla was born. When she was young, Dervla had unusual eating habits. She was allowed to eat as much fruit and cheese as she liked, but she was not allowed tea, coffee, fizzy drinks, sweets, chocolate or biscuits. For treats she would have raisins or dates. The other main things in her diet were raw beef, raw liver, raw vegetables, wholemeal bread and porridge. She drank four pints of milk a day.

As a child, she loved to read. She had a weak chest, and every winter she 'enjoyed a few weeks of invalidism ... and

> '[I've never forgotten the exact spot on a hill near my home at Lismore, County Waterford, where the decision was made and it seemed to me then, as it still seems to me now, a logical decision, based on the discoveries that cycling was a most satisfactory method of transport and that (excluding the USSR for political reasons) the way to India offered fewer watery obstacles than any other destination at a similar distance.'
>
> *Dervla Murphy*

revelled in being free to read, almost without interruption, for fourteen hours a day seven days a week'. She is still a great reader. But she didn't spend all her free time reading. Nearly every day in summer, when Dervla was a child, she would meet her father after his work and they would go swimming together in the Blackwater river.

Her mother had rheumatoid arthritis, and she became an invalid when Dervla was only a baby. The family employed a series of maids to help take care of her mother and do the housework.

Dervla's love of cycling and exploring started when she got a bicycle from her parents and an atlas from her grandfather for her tenth birthday. She became an enthusiastic cyclist.

One frosty December morning, shortly after she got her bike, she cycled to the foot of the Knockmealdown mountain, eight miles from her home, and decided to climb it. But the weather changed and she got lost in the mist. The mist turned to rain and she fell into icy water and was soaked through. Eventually, she found an old animal shelter with lots of dry bracken in it. She pulled off all her wet clothes and buried herself in the bracken to stay warm for the night. Fortunately, she was able to get home the next day to her worried parents.

When she was about twelve, Dervla went to the Ursuline boarding school in Waterford. She quite enjoyed school, but when she was fourteen she had to leave and come home to take care of her mother. It had become impossible to find help. She was her mother's full-time carer for the next sixteen years. This was difficult for the whole family.

Her mother encouraged Dervla to take breaks every now and again. So, when she was nineteen, she cycled around England and Wales on her own. Over the years she was caring for her mother, she also made short cycling trips to different countries in Europe and had some articles on her travels published in magazines and newspapers.

It wasn't until her mother died when Dervla was thirty that she was able to fulfil her childhood dream of cycling to India. (Her father was already dead by then.) This was back in the 1960s when bicycles were not as well designed as they are nowadays and there were no special comfortable cycling clothes; there were no mobile phones or GPS either. It was also a time when a woman travelling alone would have been considered to be 'asking for trouble'. Things like this did not bother Dervla – although in fact what she was doing certainly exposed her to danger at times.

She set off on her journey to India on the bike she had named Roz in one of the worst winters ever in Europe. She is a fearless traveller, but all the same she took a pistol with her.

Her daughter, Rachel, was born in 1968. Dervla was a single mother so she had to abandon her travels for a few years until Rachel was big enough to accompany her. Then the pair often travelled together and visited India, Baltistan, Peru, Madagascar and Cameroon. People used to ask her what she thought she was doing taking a defenceless girl to the wilds. Rachel survived, however, and in 2005, Dervla, Rachel and Rachel's three daughters travelled together to Cuba – though not on bicycles.

Dervla Murphy has been prepared to put up with a lot of deprivations and difficulties on her travels, and she feels her frugal rural upbringing probably helped her with this. She still lives simply and has no time for the consumer society. She has never learned to drive ('because I hate cars and I love bicycles') and one of the very few things she is afraid of is flying.

To date, Dervla Murphy has written more than twenty books. She is never afraid to express her opinions in her writing on how things are in the countries she has visited. In the 1970s she wrote a book (*A Place Apart*) about Catholics and Protestants in Northern Ireland, and her frankness resulted in her receiving threats. She continued to speak her mind in other books. For example she spoke out against nuclear power, attitudes to AIDS, apartheid, climate change and genocide.

She is an old lady now, but as recently as 2015 Dervla Murphy published *Between River and Sea*, about her experiences with Israelis and Palestinians. Her previous book, *A Month by the Sea*, was about time she spent in the Gaza Strip. She believes that it is the duty of writers to enter into the lives of the people they are writing about – and that is what makes her books so fascinating for her readers.

> Dervla is known for being fearless, both in the way she travels and in her writing. But she contradicts those who say she is courageous in the solitary journeys she makes. She maintains that, 'because in general the possibility of physical danger does not frighten me, courage is not required'.

Dervla Murphy

Fact File

1931 Born at Cappoquin, near Lismore, County Waterford.

1945 Left school to care for her mother.

1961 Dervla's mother died and Dervla could now make longer trips on her bicycle than she had been able to undertake before.

1963 Went on her first big trip, cycling all the way to India; she also spent time working with Tibetan refugee children.

1965 Her first book, *Full Tilt: Ireland to India with a Bicycle*, was published.

1965 Worked with Tibetan refugees in Nepal, an episode that she described in *The Waiting Land*, which was published in 1968.

1966 Made a trip to Ethiopia and walked with a pack mule; published *In Ethiopia with a Mule*.

1968 Her daughter Rachel was born.

Dervla Murphy

Fact File

1977 Published an account of the winter she spent with her daughter Rachel (six years old) in the sub-zero Indus Valley in Baltistan.

1978 Published *A Place Apart*, a book about Northern Ireland.

1979 Published an autobiography, *Wheels within Wheels*, describing her life up until the year she headed to India on her first long journey.

1981 Published her first political book, *Race to the Finish? The Nuclear Stakes*.

2004 Published *Through Siberia by Accident*, which describes a journey she made by train after her plans to cycle in Russia were foiled by an accident.

2005 Travelled to Cuba with her daughter and grand-daughters.

2013 Published *A Month by the Sea: Encounters in Gaza*.

2015 Published *Between River and Sea*, about time spent in Israel and Palestine.

Lelia Doolan

born 1934

An independent film-maker,
former head of light entertainment
in RTÉ and artistic director of the
Abbey Theatre, Lelia Doolan has
been a leading and controversial
figure in the arts

Lelia Doolan is best known for her work in film. She was chair of the Irish Film Board. She has lectured in film and media studies. She is herself a producer and film-maker. Her documentary film about the Northern Irish politician and activist Bernadette Devlin McAliskey won an IFTA (Irish Film and Television Academy) award in 2012.

This film, *Bernadette: Notes on a Political Journey*, was years in the making. It came out when Lelia was well past normal retirement age. But she is not a woman to have much interest in retirement. She has been working for years, into her eighties, to get the Picture Palace cinema built in Galway.

'Oh, it was lovely. There was a hot and dusty track that the cattle used leading down to the river, and a field with a sulphur well in it. We would cycle to the sea at Doolin. That is the legacy I have – a very enjoyable country childhood.'

Lelia Doolan on holidays in Clare

When Lelia Doolan was born, the family was living in County Donegal. Her mother, who was also called Lelia, went to Cork to have her baby. That was because her doctor was in Cork, where she used to live. And that's how Lelia came to be born in Cork, though she never lived there.

When the baby was born, her father sent a telegram to his wife. It said, 'Welcome to the new Lelia. Love Paddy.' And that is how our Lelia got her beautiful name.

How her mother got the name is another story. She was the last of twelve children and her parents had run out of family names, so they hunted through the Bible and the prayer-book until they found one they liked.

Lelia's parents were both from Clare and Lelia spent idyllic childhood summers there. She believes that this joyous experience

> 'Borders are interesting places. They are full of danger but also full of possibilities.'
>
> *Lelia Doolan*

at a young age has influenced her view of the world, which she has always regarded as a pleasant and welcoming place.

Lelia was considered 'delicate' as a child. Later it emerged that she is coeliac (meaning her body is unable to digest foods containing gluten, which is found in wheat and some other grains). But she says herself she was never delicate in spirit.

By the time Lelia was ready to go to school, the family was living in Dublin. She went to a small school, St Anne's in Rathgar. It was run by 'Tall Miss MacDonnell, Small Miss MacDonell, Miss Cassie and Miss Francie', as Lelia recalls. Afterwards she went on to Loreto College Beaufort and then to UCD.

After graduating from UCD, Lelia spent a year in Berlin. She was studying the work of one of the greatest European playwrights, Bertolt Brecht. This was in the days when there was East and West Germany. The city of Berlin itself was divided, with a wall between East and West Berlin. Brecht's theatre was on the East (Communist) side of the city. Lelia used to cross from West Berlin, where she lived, in order to visit the theatre.

When she came back to Ireland, Lelia worked in theatre and on a newspaper. Later she joined RTÉ and did a lot of different jobs there. After a while, she was promoted to producer/director.

She was involved, almost from the very start, in the rural soap-opera *The Riordans*. This was a hugely popular programme. Lelia had great colleagues and a lot of fun on this show.

She moved into current affairs after that and started the programme *7 Days*, the *Prime Time* of its day. This was back before cable and satellite TV. Most homes in Ireland only had RTÉ. This meant that pretty well the whole country would be watching the same programmes at the same time. *7 Days* was of central importance to the nation's awareness of world affairs. To be in charge of that programme was to have a lot of influence.

At that time, the 1960s, there were not many women in senior jobs even in a progressive area like television. RTÉ employed women as actors, present-ers and production assistants. There were also a lot of women in the design area. But technical jobs such as camera operator and senior positions like pro-ducer or director were mostly held by men. At the same time, women employed in the supporting role of production assistant were, as Lelia puts it, 'the heart and soul of the organisation'.

> 'You take chances. I think creativity is risk-taking: it's pushing the situation as far as you can and seeing what happens.'
>
> *Lelia Doolan*

Things have changed since those days and there are more opportunities now for women in TV – and there are even some men doing the formerly feminine job of production assistant.

Lelia Doolan enjoyed working in RTÉ. However, she and some of her colleagues became concerned about RTÉ policies. They thought the management was too cautious and conserva-tive. They believed that a national television station needs to be open-minded, creative and prepared to take risks. They felt this was not happening in RTÉ. In the end, Lelia and others resigned.

She ran into similar problems some years later when she was artistic director of the Abbey Theatre – the first woman to hold this position. (Lady Gregory had of course run the theatre in the early days but the position of artistic director would not have existed at that time.) Once again, the independent-mind-ed Lelia Doolan came up against a national arts organisation that she found cautious and a bit old-fashioned in its outlook. She wanted to encourage new playwrights and to put on challenging

RTÉ

As a national broadcaster RTÉ receives government funding (from the licence fee) and this is supposed to enable it to support the cultural life of the nation. On the other hand, government funding is not enough to cover costs, so RTÉ also has to rely on income from advertising. Being sandwiched between government and commercial interests can limit RTÉ's freedom and may explain a cautious outlook on the part of management.

> 'Everybody is born creative. Look at children ... they are incredible, inventive, creative, ebullient, full of fun.'
>
> *Lelia Doolan*

new work, but this was too experimental for the Abbey. She parted company with the national theatre after only a couple of years. In spite of that rather painful experience, she has always loved the Abbey and still does.

When she was in Berlin as a young woman, Lelia was supposed to be doing a master's degree, but she never finished it. After she left RTÉ, she picked up her studies again. She had always been interested in Northern Ireland. She moved to Belfast and studied anthropology in Queen's University, and got her PhD there.

She worked in theatre in Belfast too. It was the kind of drama that gave local people opportunities to write their own material for the stage. This led to exciting new plays, and Lelia very much enjoyed her time in Belfast.

She lectured on and off in film and media studies in various colleges over the years. She taught anthropology in colleges north and south of the border. She also did social research and became involved for a time in rural development, homelessness and the Combat Poverty agency.

About twenty years ago, the government wanted to build a visitor centre in the Burren in County Clare. Lelia opposed any building in this wild and beautiful place. She campaigned long and hard against this plan. Eventually the government caved in and the visitor centre was abandoned. Lelia's message from that experience is, 'Never give up if you have a cause you really believe in. And the world is more full of good people than you could possibly imagine.'

Lelia Doolan had always admired Bernadette Devlin. She followed her career when she was to the forefront in Derry and kept in touch with her when she was in prison. But then Bernadette seemed to disappear from public view. 'I didn't see Bernadette figuring in any of the discussions after the Peace Process began and I wondered where she was.'

> 'She's like a greyhound coming out of the traps.'
>
> *Lelia Doolan on Bernadette Devlin*

When Bernadette visited Galway, they made contact again. That was when Lelia had the idea of making a film about Bernadette's political career. That is the film that went on to win the IFTA award.

> 'Keep singing, keep cherishing feisty, rebellious, awkward, difficult people – that's what we're about. Cherish uncertainty, cherish failure, cherish poverty, cherish ourselves.'
>
> *From Lelia Doolan's speech on receiving the IFTA award for her film Bernadette*

Lelia Doolan has been bringing alternative film to Galway since she founded the Galway Film Fleadh in 1988. This festival has been very successful, and Lelia realised that the people of Galway are interested in seeing the kind of pictures that are not shown in the big commercial cinemas. So, along with some other people, she has worked hard to build a beautiful new 'arthouse' cinema in Galway, called the Picture Palace. It was not an easy project and it ran into financial difficulties on a couple of occasions. Lelia is very hopeful that it will be a huge success and make

> 'Without a sense of humour there is no salvation.'
>
> *Lelia Doolan*

an important contribution to the cultural life of the west of Ireland.

Lelia Doolan

Fact File

1934 Born in Cork.

LIVED in Donegal and Limerick as well as in Dublin as a child and now lives – and gardens – in County Galway.

1951–4 Studied French and German at UCD and graduated with a BA. Became interested in theatre through involvement with UCD's drama society, Dramsoc.

1955–6 Scholarship to Berlin to study the work of Bertolt Brecht.

1961 Worked freelance for RTÉ, which had just begun, as a performer, interviewer and scriptwriter. Later moved on to become a producer/director at RTÉ.

1966 Transferred from drama to current affairs at RTÉ and directed a new TV political programme, *7 Days*. (This was later replaced by *Today Tonight* and later again by *Prime Time*.)

1969 Became head of light entertainment at RTÉ, but resigned soon afterwards, along with colleagues, in protest at RTÉ policies.

1971–3 Artistic director of the Abbey Theatre. Brought in new policies to develop the work of the company, including Theatre-in-Education programme. Left after differences with management.

1974 Started graduate studies at Queen's University Belfast. Continued to live in Belfast

Lelia Doolan

Fact File

for several years, involved in community theatre.

1979–88 Lecturer and later head of communications in Rathmines College of Commerce (now part of DIT), with breaks to pursue interests in film, video and research.

1982 Got her PhD in anthropology from Queen's University Belfast.

1987 Produced Joe Comerford's film *Reefer and the Model*.

1988 Founded Galway Film Fleadh.

1993–6 Chair of Irish Film Board.

1995 Directed educational film *Ground Work*.

2011 Directed *Bernadette: Notes on a Political Journey*, a film about Bernadette Devlin McAliskey.

2012 *Bernadette* won an Irish Film and Theatre Academy award.

2018 The Picture Palace, an arthouse cinema, a project of Lelia's over several years, due to open its doors to the public.

Sr Stanislaus Kennedy

born 1939

Sr Stan has for decades been a tireless campaigner for people who are poor, especially for homeless women and children

Even as a schoolgirl Treasa Kennedy knew she wanted to work with poor families. At that time (the 1950s) there was no such job in Ireland as a social worker. When she was coming to the end of her time at school, Treasa heard about an Irish order of Catholic nuns, the Religious Sisters of Charity, who were dedicated to helping poor people.

She decided that this would be a good way for her to work with families living in poverty, and so she became a nun in that order. In those days, women were given a new name when they entered the convent, and Treasa became Sr Stanislaus.

At that time in Ireland people had not thought very much about the best way to help needy families or people who were old or sick or who had social problems, but all that was about to change.

'We were talking about things that had never been talked about before in Ireland – poverty, "unmarried mothers", care of old people. And we were doing things to make people's lives better. It was a kind of social revolution. People came to us from France, the States, the Netherlands, all over, to talk to us about what they were doing in their countries, and we learned from them. It was a very exciting time.'

Sr Stan

One person who was full of new ideas was the Catholic Bishop of Kilkenny, Dr Peter Birch – and in the early 1960s the young Sr Stanislaus was sent to Kilkenny to help Bishop Birch with his work.

At a conference on poverty in Kilkenny, Sr Stan criticised the church's attitude to poor people, and she got into trouble with her order for that. They told her not to speak in public against the church. In later years, the Sisters of Charity changed their minds and were supportive and proud of Sr Stan's work.

Sr Stanislaus started working on the problem of homelessness when she came to Dublin in the 1980s. People knew that there was some homelessness in the city. They saw older men sleeping rough on the streets.

However, Sr Stan knew there were also homeless women. It was just that women who were homeless kept it hidden. They didn't sleep rough but used hostels or they stayed with friends. During the daytime they trailed around the streets, often with their children in tow. It was a miserable life for these 'hidden homeless' women.

> 'I learnt from the women that what hurt them most was the stigma – that was worse than the cold or the hunger or anything, being looked down on and given out to and lectured.'
>
> Sr Stan

Sr Stan wanted to set up an organisation to help homeless women and their families, but first she decided that she needed to understand the problem. She thought the best plan was to listen to the women themselves and try to find out how to help them.

So she got a group of homeless women together and spent a lot of time with them, learning from them about their lives. She found out what kinds of problems they had and what they needed to help them to move out of homelessness and get back to living more normal lives. This may seem a perfectly logical way to go about things, but at that time it was an amazing new idea.

When Sr Stan's new organisation, Focus Point (later renamed Focus Ireland), opened its doors in 1985, it provided exactly the things those women had told her they needed: a warm, safe place to go during the day for a cup of coffee and something to eat; a phone line they could ring if they needed advice; friendly people who could give them information and help them to find answers to their problems. Ever since, Sr Stan's way of working

Mother Mary Aikenhead

During the 19th and 20th centuries, nuns played an important role in Irish life. Women who got married were expected to stay at home and look after their families. But orders of nuns founded and ran schools and hospitals.

Mary Aikenhead founded the Religious Sisters of Charity in 1815. Until then, most nuns in Ireland lived in enclosed convents (meaning that they stayed in their convents and did not have much contact with the outside world). Mary Aikenhead's new order was the first one where the sisters went out to work among the poor in their own homes.

Mother Mary Aikenhead was utterly committed to helping poor people, and she has always been an inspiration to Sr Stan in her life as a nun and an activist for the poor.

Unmarried mothers

In the past in Ireland, unmarried women who had babies
had a very difficult time. They were often rejected by
their families, and many of them were sent to mother-
and-baby homes that were run by nuns. The babies
were usually given up for adoption. In some cases,
there were laundries attached to these homes, called
'Magdalene laundries'. The women had to work in the
laundries, often with little or no pay.

That is how Irish society at the time dealt with a social
issue that it considered shameful. Attitudes have
changed in recent years, and there has been a lot of
public anger about the conditions in mother-and-baby
homes and Magdalene laundries. As a result, many
orders of nuns have been involved in public controversy.

When Sr Stan started to research homelessness in
the 1980s, she included older women who had been
'unmarried mothers' and were still living in convents
years later. It was thought strange at that time to call
such people homeless, but Sr Stan's thinking was that
having a roof over your head is not the same as having a
place that is really a home.

has been to listen to people and to try to provide what it is that they need, instead of providing what the system thinks they should have.

Today, Focus Ireland has grown into a big organisation. It provides homeless people all over Ireland with housing. It also helps people who are moving out of homelessness to settle in their new homes and it goes on supporting them if they need it.

In the 1990s, Sr Stan became aware that Ireland was changing once more. It had always been a country of emigration, but now the economy was booming, and there was so much work that we needed people to come and do some of it for us. Sr Stan set up the Immigrant Council of Ireland to help people who were coming to work in Ireland to get their legal and human rights.

Sr Stan believes that young people are full of ideas, enthusiasm and compassion, and that is why she founded Young Social Innovators. This is a programme that encourages young people in secondary schools to think about social problems and to come up with ideas to solve them.

Another radical idea Sr Stan had is that children and young people can learn and enjoy mindfulness and meditation. The centre for meditation that she started in Dublin, The Sanctuary, has a programme for children.

Especially in the earlier part of her working life, Sr Stan worked in an Ireland where women's voices were not always heard, and certainly the voices of poor women were not listened to. As a nun, she was often able to get men in authority to listen to her, and she was never afraid to ask rich and powerful people for things, not for herself but for poor people – and sometimes she got what she asked for.

It is a great source of sadness to her that the homelessness problem in Ireland has got worse and worse, but she and the organisations she set up over the course of her working life have made life better for thousands of voiceless people.

Sr Stan

Fact File

1939 Born Treasa Kennedy into a farming family in Rinn Buí near Lispole on the Dingle Peninsula in County Kerry.

SPOKE Irish as well as English growing up.

1957 Became a Sister of Charity and took the name Stanislaus.

1960s/70s With Bishop Peter Birch, developed and helped provide social services in Kilkenny.

1985 Founded Focus Point (later Focus Ireland), an organisation that helps homeless people to find a way out of homelessness and provides supported housing all over Ireland.

1997 Appointed to the Council of State by President Mary McAleese.

1998 Published her first book on spirituality, *Now Is the Time*.

1998 Set up The Sanctuary, a centre in Dublin for meditation and mindfulness.

2001 Set up the Immigrant Council of Ireland, which helps immigrants to Ireland with legal and human rights advice (www. immigrantcouncil.ie), and Young Social Innovators Ireland, which encourages young people at school to come up with projects of social value.

2016 Published *Mindful Meditations for Every Day*.

2017 Awarded honorary doctorate by Dublin City University.

Mary Robinson

born 1944

**Mary Robinson, lawyer
and campaigner for human
rights, was Ireland's first
female president**

As a young woman, Mary Robinson was a very brilliant student, and was made Reid Professor of Law at Trinity College Dublin when she was only twenty-five. She was also active in politics around that time, and she was elected a senator representing graduates of Trinity.

Especially when she was young, Mary got into trouble with the church for some of her views. It was hard for people to disagree publicly with church views at that time, and it took a certain kind of bravery to stand up for a different point of view, as Mary Robinson did. The local parish priest in her home town of Ballina said harsh things about her in public, at Mass. That was very difficult for her family.

Her family was also unhappy that Mary had married a Protestant. (Her husband, Nicholas Robinson, is a member of the Church of Ireland.) In those days, marrying across the religious divide was badly thought of (by both religions) and could cause real anxiety and sadness for families. (The rift between Mary Robinson and her family has long since been healed.)

In the 1970s, there was a surge in feminist activism in Ireland, led by journalists such as June Levine, Nell McCafferty and Mary Maher. Mary Robinson supported their objectives through her work as a lawyer and a senator. She used her position in the Seanad (senate) to change the law and improve women's rights, and she worked to get contraception legalised. She also

> The President of Ireland (Uachtarán na hÉireann) is the official head of state (a bit like a king or queen in some countries) and is not the head of the government (unlike in the United States, for example). This means that the president does not have much political power. However, the president can have a lot of influence in other ways.

Discrimination against women in Ireland

The Ireland in which Mary Robinson grew up was very conservative. The Catholic church had a strong influence, and both the law of the land and people's social attitudes reflected Catholic thinking.

There was no divorce, and women whose husbands were violent, for example, were expected to put up with it. Many women had more children than they wanted to have or could afford to bring up, and contraception was illegal. Unmarried women who had babies often had to give them up for adoption, even if they wanted to keep them. There was no social welfare payment for an unmarried woman with a child.

Women did not have equal rights with men. For example, women were paid much less than men, even when they did the same work. When they got married, women who worked in government-controlled jobs (such as teachers and civil servants) and in some private companies had to leave their jobs. Women were not secure even in their own homes: a husband was allowed to sell the family home even if his wife did not agree. Women were not allowed to serve on juries – which meant that even in rape cases all the jurors were men.

championed prisoners' rights and was active in favour of Ireland joining the EEC (now the EU).

Until quite recent times, it was against the law to be gay, or at least to behave that way, in Ireland. Mary Robinson was a member of the Campaign for Homosexual Law Reform. In 1977, a politician called David Norris took a court case to try to make the state legalise homosexuality. Mary Robinson was his barrister. Norris and Robinson lost their case in 1983. David Norris then took the case to the European Court of Human Rights. The European court ruled in favour of Norris in 1988, and eventually, in 1993, the Irish law was changed.

When the Labour Party (together with other left-wing organisations) asked Mary Robinson, in 1989, if they could nominate her as a candidate for the presidency, such an idea had never even crossed her mind. But she accepted, and she went on to be elected Ireland's first female president. All the men who had been president before her had either been members of the Fianna Fáil party or had been supported by that party. It was a huge change for Ireland to have a dynamic woman and a person who was known for her feminist and liberal social views as president.

> 'I must be a president for all the people, but more than that, I *want* to be a president for all the people. Because I was elected by men and women of all parties and none, by many with great moral courage, who stepped out from the faded flags of the Civil War and voted for a new Ireland, and above all by the women of Ireland, *mná na hÉireann*, who instead of rocking the cradle, rocked the system.'
>
> *Mary Robinson*

In her inaugural speech, Mary Robinson thanked Irish women for their support and she invited people to 'come dance with me in Ireland'. This quotation from an old poem (made famous by WB Yeats) set a warm and joyous tone for her presidency. She went on to be a much more visible president and one who engaged more with people than had been usual in the past.

She adapted the Irish custom of putting a lighted candle in the window at Christmas as a sign of welcome. She placed a light in the window of Áras an Uachtaráin (the official home of the president) every night, to remember Irish emigrants all over the world.

She was the first Irish president to meet an English monarch when she met Queen Elizabeth II. Relations between Ireland and the United Kingdom had not always been friendly, because of our history and especially because of the troubles in Northern Ireland, so this was an important meeting. She also shook hands with Gerry Adams, head of Sinn Féin. This was at a time when Sinn Féin representatives weren't allowed to speak on Irish radio and television. For the president to make this gesture at that time was very controversial.

'As an advocate for the hungry and the hunted, the forgotten and the ignored, Mary Robinson has not only shone a light on human suffering but illuminated a better future for our world.'

Barrack Obama, 2009

Mary Robinson has always been a champion not just of women's rights but of global human rights. She wanted to 'shine a light' on Africa's problems. She was the first head of state to visit Somalia after its civil war and famine and later Rwanda after its terrible genocide.

As she was coming towards the end of her term as President of Ireland, Mary Robinson was appointed High Commissioner for Human Rights by the United Nations. As she had always done, she expressed her views as High Commissioner, even when they were controversial. Once again she got into trouble, especially – but not only – for criticising the United States.

Since stepping down as High Commissioner in 2002, Mary Robinson has continued to work for social justice internationally, and especially for people affected by climate change. The organisation she set up in Dublin in 2010, the Mary Robinson Foundation – Climate Justice, works to 'secure global justice' for people who are 'usually forgotten – the poor, the disempowered and the marginalised across the world'.

Mary McAleese

Mary Robinson was followed, in 1997, by Ireland's second woman president, Mary McAleese. Mary McAleese was the first woman in the world to become president immediately after another woman. She grew up in Northern Ireland, and was the first Northerner to be President of Ireland.

Like Mary Robinson, Mary McAleese was a lawyer and had been Reid Professor of Law at Trinity College Dublin. Also like Mary Robinson, Mary McAleese is interested in social justice and equality. As a Northerner, she is particularly opposed to sectarianism, and as president she wanted to 'build bridges' with Northern communities, especially with unionists. Her most important achievement as president was her contribution to the Northern Irish Peace Process.

She was a popular president and served two terms (1997–2011).

Mary Robinson

Fact File

1944 Born Mary Bourke, in Ballina, County Mayo, into a medical family – both her parents were doctors – as the middle child and the only girl in a family of five.

1967 Graduated from Trinity College Dublin with a law degree and went to Harvard University in the United States to take up a scholarship and study further.

1969 Appointed Reid Professor of Constitutional and Criminal Law at Trinity College, the youngest professor of law in the country.

1969–89 Served in Seanad Éireann, representing Trinity graduates, mostly as an independent, though she was a member of the Labour Party from 1977 to 1981.

1970 Married Nicholas Robinson (and went on to have three children).

1977–83 Acted as barrister for David Norris in his case against the state on the law that outlawed homosexuality.

1979–83 Served on Dublin City Council and was active in a campaign to save an important Viking site at Wood Quay in Dublin; the campaign was unsuccessful and the City Council built office blocks on top of one of the most important archaeological sites in Europe.

Mary Robinson

Fact File

1990–97 Served as Uachtarán na hÉireann – President of Ireland – the first woman to hold this position.

1992 Visited Somalia after the civil war and famine there.

1997 Visited Rwanda after the terrible genocide there.

1997–2002 Served as United Nations High Commissioner for Human Rights.

1998 Appointed Chancellor of Trinity College Dublin; like the presidency of Ireland, this is mostly a ceremonial role but one with influence.

2002–10 Worked with an organisation she set up, Realizing Rights – The Ethical Globalization Initiative, an organisation that aimed to make globalisation work better for people by promoting fairer trade and establishing people's right to decent working conditions and health.

2009 Awarded the Presidential Medal of Freedom, the highest civilian honour awarded by the United States.

2010 Set up the Mary Robinson Foundation – Climate Justice.

Bernadette Devlin McAliskey

born 1947

Bernadette Devlin was an icon of the Civil Rights movement in Northern Ireland in the 1960s and now works as a community activist

The Northern Irish political activist Bernadette Devlin McAliskey has been a controversial figure all her life. When she was young she supported people who fought against police violence. In recent years she has defended migrant workers who face prejudice, and she campaigns for women's rights. She describes herself as both a socialist and a feminist. Especially when she was young, her radicalism often put her in dangerous situations. She told one journalist: 'I look back on myself then and I am astounded I survived. I made mad decisions.'

Bernadette Devlin was raised in a Catholic family in County Tyrone. At home she was taught the ideal of universal solidarity, meaning that people should all care for and help each other. She says that she learned to be strong from her mother and grandmother, who were both widows: 'I come from a long line of strong women.'

The Northern Ireland in which Bernadette grew up was (and still is) very divided between unionists (who want to remain part of the UK and are mostly Protestants) and nationalists (who want a united Ireland and are nearly all Catholics). At that time, it was difficult for nationalists to get certain jobs or council houses in Northern Ireland. This was because the unionists (who were the majority population) held all the power and influence. Elections were often unfair and the police, who nearly all came from the unionist community, could be hostile or even violent to people they were meant to protect.

Because of her background and because of the causes she has been involved with, Bernadette Devlin is often seen as a republican (extreme nationalist) figure. But it might be more accurate to say that she was a socialist first and a republican second. She believed in republican politics but did not actively support violence. As a young woman, she became convinced that the problem in Northern Ireland wasn't just prejudice between the two communities but lay in the economic system. She believed the system

When she was elected to parliament, Bernadette Devlin was considered a dangerous communist. She was described by a Unionist MP as 'Fidel Castro in a mini-skirt'. This was supposed to be a put-down, but depending on your point of view, it could also be regarded as a badge of honour.

Fidel Castro was a Marxist revolutionary and dictator of the communist state of Cuba; and of course the young Bernadette Devlin wore mini-skirts, as did many women of her age at the time.

put money and profit before the needs of ordinary people. She felt that poor people were badly treated whether they were Catholic or Protestant, nationalist or unionist.

She won a scholarship to study psychology at Queen's University Belfast. While there, she helped to found the radical civil rights organisation People's Democracy. During one People's Democracy march she saw police beating unarmed students who had been protesting. Before she could finish her degree, she lost her scholarship and was expelled for 'bringing the university into disrepute'.

In April 1969 when she was just twenty-one, she stood for election in the Mid-Ulster constituency as a 'Unity' candidate – a term that refers to an electoral pact between various nationalist and left-wing candidates. She won the election and became Westminster's youngest (and fieriest) female MP. At that time, Northern Irish republicans who were elected to parliament did not take their seats, as a protest against British rule. But Bernadette Devlin was her own woman and she took her seat. Her first speech in parliament was much more radical than most people expected from a new MP:

There is no place in society for us, the ordinary 'peasants' of Northern Ireland. There is no place for us in the society of landlords because we are the 'have-nots' and they are the 'haves'.

Later that year she toured the United States to raise money for the Northern Irish civil rights movement. She appeared on popular television shows such as *Meet the Press* and *The Johnny Carson Show*. While she was there she offered her support to the American civil rights movement. She challenged Irish Americans to see the similarities between the mistreatment of Northern Irish nationalists and black Americans.

In that same year, 1969, the Northern Irish 'troubles' broke out – meaning the violent conflict that lasted for thirty years and killed thousands of people. Bernadette Devlin helped to organise the nationalist community in Derry in the 'Battle of the Bogside'. The Bogside, a Catholic area of Derry, had come under siege by the police and the B-Specials (a section of the British army) after rioting in Derry city. The successful three-day defence of the Bogside was organised by local leaders, including Bernadette Devlin. She was sentenced to six months in prison as a result, for 'incitement to riot'.

Bernadette Devlin's daughter Róisín was born in 1971. Bernadette was not married. At that time, having a baby outside of marriage was still very much disapproved of. Bernadette lost some support because of this. She married Róisín's father, Michael McAliskey, two years later, and they had two more children.

In 1972 a civil rights march was held in Derry. Bernadette Devlin was there, and was to give a speech. British paratroopers (a particular kind of soldier) opened fire on the unarmed protesters, killing thirteen people and wounding over a dozen more. This dreadful day came to be known as Bloody Sunday. It has become one of the most notorious events in the history of Northern Ireland.

At the time, the British government supported the army and insisted that soldiers had only opened fire in response to being shot at. It was nearly forty years before a British prime minister, David Cameron, admitted: 'What happened on Bloody Sunday was both unjustified and unjustifiable. It was wrong.'

Because she had been present at the event, Bernadette Devlin was entitled to give an eye-witness account in parliament, but she was not allowed to speak. When the British home secretary claimed that the soldiers had only fired in self-defence, she walked across the floor of the House of Commons and slapped him in the face, shouting 'Murderous hypocrite!'

(Unless you count that slap) Bernadette Devlin never became involved in violence herself. But in 1981 she supported Irish republican prisoners in the H-Blocks of the Long Kesh (Maze) prison. These prisoners were on hunger strike because they claimed they were political prisoners and not criminals.

Perhaps in response to her support for the hunger-strikers, loyalist (unionist extremist) paramilitaries broke into the McAliskeys' home and shot Bernadette and her husband in front of their children. She was very badly wounded and thought she might die. However, a British army doctor arrived and brought them to hospital.

After that, the family had to move to a different estate in Coalisland, County Tyrone, for their safety. In this new area, Bernadette began to work with other local women to found a community group to deal with social issues. She did twice run (unsuccessfully) for election to the Dáil in the Republic of Ireland, but apart from that, she has now made community activism the focus of her life.

Violence in Northern Ireland came to an end with the signing of the Good Friday Agreement in 1998. However, it is an uneasy peace. Bernadette believes that the divisions in Northern Ireland will only heal properly when people from different communities start to desegregate, live and work together in mixed communities and get to know each other better. She has argued that helping people out of poverty and making society fairer is the only thing that can guarantee peace in the long term.

In 1997 she co-founded STEP (the South Tyrone Empowerment Programme) to help people who are marginalised – migrants, single parents, Travellers, people with intellectual disabilities. In recent years she has spoken out for the rights of workers, migrants and refugees. She has worked with unionists as well as nationalists to narrow the divide between the two communities.

Bernadette Devlin McAliskey's daughter Róisín also became a radical political activist and in 1996 was almost extradited to Germany, when she was accused of helping the IRA to attack a British army base there. Róisín was held in prison and badly treated even though she was pregnant at the time. Bernadette argued that Róisín was innocent, and she was eventually released.

Bernadette Devlin

Fact File

1947 Born Bernadette Devlin in Cookstown, County Tyrone.

1969 Elected to parliament in Westminster; she was the youngest ever female MP until the 2015 election.

1969 Served six months in prison for taking part in the Battle of the Bogside.

1969 Published her autobiography *The Price of My Soul*.

1970 Elected as an independent socialist.

1971 Had her daughter Róisín.

1973 Married Róisín's father, Michael McAliskey; she went on to have two other children, Deirdre and Fintan.

1974 Helped found the Irish Republican Socialist Party.

1981 She and her husband were shot and badly wounded in their home by loyalist (militant unionist) paramilitaries.

1997 Co-founded STEP, the South Tyrone Empowerment Programme (www.stepni.org), to help marginalised people.

2003 Barred from entering the United States as she 'posed a risk to national security'.

Garry Hynes

born 1953

Garry Hynes is a leading theatre director with an international reputation

The first woman ever to win a Tony Award – Broadway's equivalent of the Oscars – for theatre direction was an Irishwoman, Garry Hynes, for directing Martin McDonagh's *The Beauty Queen of Leenane*. That was in 1998. By then, Garry Hynes had been directing plays for twenty-five years. She joined the Drama Society when she was studying in University College Galway (now called NUIG). She was attracted to the idea of being involved in drama, but she didn't want to act – and so she more or less fell into directing.

As Garry's college days were coming to an end, she knew she didn't want to lose her involvement in drama, which had become very important to her. So, with two actor friends, Mick Lally and Marie Mullen, she founded the Druid Theatre Company where they lived, in Galway city. Decades later, Druid has put on plays around the world, but its home has always been in Galway. You could think of it as a theatre company with a west of Ireland accent.

Indeed, Garry Hynes has a west of Ireland accent herself. She grew up in Ballaghaderreen, County Roscommon (where her father was principal of the local vocational school) and later lived in Galway. Her family spoke Irish at home, and it was only when she went to school that the young Garry learned English. When she was small, she found it frustrating not being able to communicate with other children. She rebelled against the family ethic of speaking Irish and once she learned English she became less fluent in Irish. However, her bilingual childhood has left her with an interest in language.

As a child she was a voracious reader. She remembers that before she learned to read, she longed to be able to decipher print. She tried to get into the adult section of the public library when she was still a child. The librarian chased her back to the children's library. The nearest adult books to the children's were in the poetry section – and so she started to read poetry at a

Winning a Tony Award

'When I got the nomination people started to say that I could be the first and I couldn't believe that a woman hadn't won it yet. These awards were more than fifty years old and I was very aware of the role that women had played in 20th-century Irish and American theatre. Some of the great lighting designers and directors were women. Shows on Broadway are all about finance, and finance was then and is still relentlessly male.

'I was very proud that I was the first woman, but I was aware while being proud that there were loads of women before me who should have won if the context had been different.'

Garry Hynes

Waking the Feminists (2016)

The centenary of the 1916 Rising was celebrated with events all over the country. The national theatre, the Abbey, published its 2016 programme, 'Waking the Nation', in 2015. This programme had very few women playwrights on it. Women involved in theatre in Ireland were incensed. Their response was to set up a campaign which they named 'Waking the Feminists'.

The first Waking the Feminists meeting was held in the Abbey Theatre itself in November 2015. This was followed by meetings all over the country, and the campaign gathered energy and support. The final meeting was held, again in the Abbey Theatre, a year after the first meeting.

Waking the Feminists made people aware of how few women artists were doing well, not just in the Abbey but in Irish theatre generally. The Arts Council published a study called *Gender Counts*, which showed that it was true that women were not succeeding as well as they should in Irish theatre. As Lian Bell, founder and leader of the campaign, put it: 'The idea that women will get there on their own merit was rubbish because they haven't ... there's something stopping women getting through.'

When people talked about the issue, it became clear that the problem was not so much deliberate discrimination against women as a kind of unconscious bias. When this was pointed out, most people were concerned to try to put things right. The Abbey Theatre set up a committee to make sure that women artists are properly represented in their programmes in the future.

'In twelve short months Waking the Feminists has fundamentally changed the Irish theatre community,' says Lian Bell. 'That's not something anyone imagined was possible ... Like never before, we are respectfully but firmly insisting we be listened to.'

young age. She was an expert on English inter-war poetry in her teens!

When she became involved in theatre in college she started to read plays, and her interest in drama exploded. She would go to New York in the summers and there she saw the kinds of productions you would never see in Ireland at that time – plays made by young people playing to young audiences. It was a combination of that excitement about theatre that she discovered in New York and her experience of working in theatre as a student that inspired her to found Druid.

The first play that Druid did was JM Synge's *The Playboy of the Western World*. That play has been a cornerstone of their repertoire ever since. Garry Hynes and Druid have put it on many times in many different places, including in New York. They went on to create the monumental DruidSynge in 2005 – a production of all six of Synge's plays in a single day. DruidSynge toured the United States and was described by the *New York Times* theatre critic as 'the highlight not just of my theatregoing year but of my theatregoing life'.

'We were a bunch of young people just out of college doing plays in a Jesuit hall and then in a function room in the back of a hotel. We began to realise that we had to attract an audience, so we started putting on lunch time theatre. People might try that out if it was only forty minutes long.

'Developing a community was a big part of it. People started bringing their old clothes and props to us. We had a bit of an innocence about the right way or wrong way to do things. We found out how to do them together with our audience. We weren't to know it at the time but looking back on it it was liberating.'

Garry Hynes

Druid has had a long-standing relationship with the Galway playwright Tom Murphy, and DruidSynge was followed in 2013 by DruidMurphy (consisting of a trilogy of Murphy's plays). Druid also looks beyond Irish playwrights: DruidSynge and DruidMurphy were followed in 2015 by DruidShakespeare, a production of several of Shakespeare's history plays.

In 1990 Garry Hynes left Druid and became artistic director of the Abbey Theatre. This was a totally different experience – moving from a dynamic young independent theatre company to a national institution. She found it very challenging.

It wasn't until she started at the Abbey that Garry became aware of the difficulties that women working in the theatre face. She found that if a man behaved in a certain way, that behaviour was explained in one way; if a woman behaved in the same way, it was viewed very differently. It was accepted that a man could be ambitious, for example, but that would be seen as extraordinary in a woman.

She left the Abbey after a few years, but looking back on the experience, she is very glad that she did it. She came back to Druid with a renewed sense of commitment to her own company.

Her view on the Waking the Feminists movement is that it has

'Looking at it from the point of view of a headcount is not the solution. The fact is that 80% of the canon of modern theatre going back 500 years is written by men. You can't suddenly stop performing that because if you do you disconnect from something that is fundamental to theatre. At the same time you have to encourage women. So I think it's complex and not a short process.'

Garry Hynes on Waking the Feminists

> 'You have to have a strong belief in your idea but if you have only a strong belief then you don't have the necessary doubt that will strengthen any idea. You have to be able to doubt, engage with the doubts, and then say well even if I am doubtful I'm still going to go ahead. If you're just a bully it doesn't work either.'
>
> *Garry Hynes*

been a valuable and necessary wake-up call for everyone. She has always believed that everything men could do, women could do too. Compared to the lives of previous generations, women today have far more opportunities, but a lot of work had to be done to make that progress. Achieving equality for women in theatre is not something that can be done overnight, in her view.

She believes that the way to make progress and bring about change is by connecting with other people and persuading them that what you are trying to do is right.

Garry Hynes has been aware that she is gay since she was in her teens. Coming out was not easy for her, because she did not want to upset her parents. She is very aware that being gay is easier for her as a person working in the arts. Had she been a teacher, for example, living in small-town Ireland, it would have been much more dificult. She points out that coming out is not something that you just do once and then it's over – when you are gay, you never stop coming out; you have to tell new people all the time.

Asked if she thinks she would have had a different experience in life and in the theatre if she had not been a woman, her unhesitating answer is: 'I've no doubt whatsoever I would – a much less rich experience than the one I've had.'

Garry Hynes

Fact File

1953 Born Margaret Geraldine Mary Hynes, called Gearóidín, later shorted to Garry by friends, the eldest of four children (two boys and two girls), in Ballaghaderreen, County Roscommon; her father was principal in the local vocational school and the family spoke Irish at home.

EDUCATED in St Louis Convent in Monaghan and Taylor's Hill in Galway.

1971–4 Studied English and History at UCG.

1975 With Mick Lally and Marie Mullen founded the Druid Theatre Company whose first production she directed – JM Synge's *The Playboy of the Western World*.

1975–91 Director of Druid.

1980 Druid triumphed with a series of plays at the Edinburgh Fringe Festival at The Bedlam theatre.

1982 Druid appeared for the first time in the Dublin Theatre Festival with Hynes's production of Synge's *The Playboy of the Western World*.

1986 Started to direct for the Abbey Theatre. Her first work there was *Whistle in the Dark* by Tom Murphy.

1990 Appointed artistic director of the Abbey Theatre.

1991 Controversial production at the Abbey of novelist John McGahern's play *The Power of Darkness*.

1995 Came back to Druid as director and is currently still in that position.

DRUID premiered Martin McDonagh's *The Beauty Queen of Leenane*, in a co-production with the Royal Court Theatre.

Garry Hynes

Fact File

1998 First woman to win a Tony Award for direction, for *The Beauty Queen of Leenane.*

1998 Received an honorary doctorate from the National University of Ireland.

2001 Received honorary doctorate in literature from University College Dublin.

2002 Received *The Irish Times/* ESB Irish Theatre Award for Best Director for *Big Maggie* by John B Keane at the Abbey.

2003 Again won *The Irish Times* Theatre Award for Christina Reilly's *The Good Father* and John B Keane's *Sive.*

2004 Received an honorary doctorate from the University of Dublin (Trinity College).

2005 Won *The Irish Times* Special Tribute Award for her contribution to Irish theatre.

2005 Directed DruidSynge, a critically acclaimed production of all six of John Millington Synge's plays; this has since toured to Dublin, Edinburgh, Inis Meáin, Minneapolis and New York.

2006 Awarded the Freedom of the City of Galway.

DIRECTED *Translations* by Brian Friel, which transferred to Broadway in 2007.

2013 Directed DruidMurphy – a trilogy of Tom Murphy plays.

2015 Directed DruidShakespeare – four Shakespearean histories, which won *The Irish Times* Theatre Award for Best Production in 2017.

2017 Awarded Honorary Fellowship of the Royal College of Physicians of Ireland.

Paula Meehan

born 1955

Paula Meehan is one of Ireland's leading poets and an activist on behalf of working-class communities

When she was small, Paula Meehan lived mostly with her grandparents, because her parents travelled back and forth to London a lot for work. Her grandparents lived 'in town', as Dubliners call the centre of the city.

When she was still in primary school, Paula found out that writing poetry can get you into trouble. She was supposed to write a three-page essay for homework, but instead she handed up a poem. Her dog had died and she was feeling very sad, so that was why she wrote the poem. Her teacher thought she was just trying to get out of writing a long essay and was very cross with her. 'But my dog was *dead*!' she protested.

> 'I believe poems are mirrors: we see ourselves in them.'
>
> *Paula Meehan*

After her parents moved back permanently to Ireland, Paula lived with them in Finglas, a large suburb north of Dublin city. 'We had a great youth culture there in the sixties,' Paula says. 'Bands, music, writing songs. We were part of what was happening all over the world at the time. I loved it. It was a great time to be young.'

Paula was able to go to secondary school, because free secondary education had just started in Ireland around the time she left primary school. She got into trouble at secondary school when she led a protest against the school rules and she

> 'It's important to know that if something goes wrong for you in life, in education for example, you can find another way. Nowadays there are lots of opportunities for second-chance education: you can go to college later in life if you want to, so there is no need to let a setback ruin your life.'
>
> *Paula Meehan*

> 'Having a supportive family is everything. If you have that, you can survive catastrophes. My grandparents told me all the time how wonderful I was. Every child needs that, to feel they are the centre of the universe. That is what gives you faith in yourself, and you need that in life.'
>
> *Paula Meehan*

was expelled. Getting expelled from school might sound very heroic, but looking back on it, Paula knows that her life could have gone very badly wrong at that point.

However, this experience taught her to be self-sufficient. She just went and found out what the curriculum was and studied it herself and passed her exams anyway. They let her back into the school to do her inter cert (same as junior cert today), but they made her sit all by herself, cordoned off from everyone else. 'It was humiliating. I really was in deep trouble.' She now has a good relationship with her old school, and is very happy that they are planning to use some lines of her poetry in an art garden that the transition year students there are creating.

Luckily, Paula had the support of her family at that difficult time. Her mother helped her to find a place in another school afterwards, and she got a great education there. They even put on Latin classes especially for her because they knew she wanted to go to university. (In those days you needed to have Latin for most university courses.)

When she was fifteen, Paula had her first poem published in a local youth magazine. She found it an overwhelming experience, and she didn't publish another poem for many years after that.

Paula was the first person from her family or her community to go to university. In those days, it was nearly impossible to find people from a background like Paula's in Trinity College. But

Non-Stop Connolly Show

'I got my history from John Arden and Margaretta D'Arcy's *Non-Stop Connolly Show*. This was a series of six plays about the life of James Connolly, and it was put on in Liberty Hall over a twenty-four-hour period. It was history from the point of view of the working class, the underdogs; it was the history of my people.

'We rehearsed for three months. I was sort of apprenticed to a very skilled woman who knew all about making masks and puppets, even props, and she taught me lots. We used papier maché and glue size. It was great. I loved doing that. I got to make a puppet of Queen Victoria, three times life size, and I made her crown – a tiara – out of skulls, for the Famine Queen. That was the first time I experienced the healing power of art.'

Paula Meehan

> 'Going to Trinity – it was a bit like Harry Potter going to Hogwarts, all those beautiful buildings, and lots of nooks and crannies – mysterious and amazing.'
>
> *Paula Meehan*

she made lots of friends, and the main thing she learnt at college was how to get on with people from all kinds of backgrounds and all sorts of places.

She was not always very good at going to her lectures, though. She studied Greek drama and mythology, and she never missed any of those lectures, because she loved those stories. But she skipped most of her history lectures, because she could not see her own history there. She was to be found 'in other haunts around the city' during history lectures.

Paula was involved in protest movements while she was a student. The most important issue at the time for her was the protest against building a nuclear power station at Carnsore Point in County Wexford. 'Even the guards who were patrolling the protests agreed with us in the end that building a nuclear power station on a small, beautiful island was not a good idea. And in the end, we won!'

Paula was writing poems all the time she was in college, but in secret. She didn't feel comfortable in the world of poetry in Ireland at that time. Poets were mostly male. Female poets – such as Eavan Boland, who wrote about what it was like to be a woman – were often not highly rated by the men. For example, when *The Field Day Anthology of*

> 'There was a kind of priesthood of beardy old poets in pubs off Grafton Street. I really didn't feel I had anything to do with them.'
>
> *Paula Meehan*

Irish Writing, supposed to represent the best Irish writers, came out in 1991 – more than a decade after Paula Meehan left college – there were hardly any woman writers in it.

After leaving Trinity, Paula decided that she needed to get out of Ireland for a while. She wanted to study creative writing, and she won a scholarship to go to Eastern Washington University in the United States. (This is in Washington state, in the 'wild northwest' of America, not Washington DC where the White House is.) She spent a wonderful two years there, writing poetry and working with professional poets that she admired. She was very impressed with the Native American culture that she found there, especially among the Haida Coastal People. She loved their stories about deer and salmon and shape-changing, which reminded her of our own ancient stories here in Ireland.

When Paula Meehan returned to Dublin in the 1980s after her time in the United States, she found that her city had totally changed. There was a dreadful economic recession, and heroin had hit the population in the streets where she had grown up. With heroin addiction came AIDS, and people's lives were devastated – children were starving, their parents sick and strung out.

The poet and Trinity professor Brendan Kennelly saw that Paula was full of anger about what was happening to her community, and he suggested to her that she might do some

> Speaking of Paula Meehan's poems, the poet Eavan Boland remarked, 'Look at me, they seem to say to a reader, your world is not lost here. This poem gives it back to you. It will in fact bind you more closely to it.'

'The Statue of the Virgin at Granard Speaks'

It is not very long ago since having a baby outside marriage was considered a dreadful thing in Ireland. An unmarried girl who got pregnant would very often be so scared of being found out that she would keep her pregnancy a secret.

A fifteen-year-old girl called Ann Lovett had a baby in 1984. She told no-one she was pregnant and she gave birth alone, out of doors in the cold, in a grotto, under a statue of the Virgin Mary. She died and so did her baby. Paula Meehan wrote a poem about this terrible event called 'The Statue of the Virgin at Granard Speaks'. It is one of her most famous poems.

work in the prisons. She took his advice and started doing poetry workshops with women prisoners. It was tough work and very emotional, and in the end she had to give it up because she was burnt out by it. Nowadays, she works with an organisation called RADE (Recovery through Art, Drama and Education) which gives people who are recovering from addiction the opportunity to work with art and drama. This suits Paula very well – she is a poet whose work is very much grounded in her sense of community.

'It's not about teaching people – it's about making work with people, and it allows people to explore their own creative power. ... This kind of work is so important and so healing, but it is totally underfunded. I don't know why that is, but it makes me angry.'

Paula Meehan, on her work with RADE

It was not until she came back from studying in America that Paula had her first book of poems published. She went on to publish books of poems over the years with a variety of publishers in Ireland and Britain. As well as writing poetry, Paula has continued to be involved in drama, and she has written several plays.

The poem printed here, 'The Quilt', was inspired by a memory of sleeping in her grandmother's house in Marino, where they lived when Paula was a teenager. She also means this poem as a tribute to the people from her community who have died as a result of addiction, like the memorial quilts that people make to remember AIDS victims.

She was very honoured to be made Ireland Professor of Poetry in 2013. This is the Irish equivalent of Poet Laureate, and lasts for three years. Paula feels happiest, she says, at a point

The Quilt

It was a simple affair – nine squares
by nine squares, blue on green spots, stripes, bows
alternate with gold and red chevrons:
my grandmother's quilt I slept under
the long and winding nights of childhood.

Above the bed, a roundy window
my own full moon. I loved the weathers
wheeling past, the stars, the summer suns;
my aunties' deep breaths, distant thunder.

from Geomantic © *Paula Meehan 2016*
by kind permission of the poet and Dedalus Press

Count how many lines there are in this poem. And now
count how many syllables there are in each line. Does that
remind you of anything?

There are eighty other poems (9x9=81) on the exact same
pattern in Paula Meehan's collection *Geomantic*.

somewhere between the university and the street – and being Professor of Poetry gave her the chance to bring those two parts of her life together.

Paula Meehan is very concerned about women's rights and about the rights of people from poor backgrounds. Things have improved in many ways in recent years in Ireland, but Paula knows there is still a lot of prejudice, and there is a constant battle to be fought against it.

'People don't always speak out their prejudice these days – it's not cool to be prejudiced – but they have ways of letting people know they think they are not good enough. They speak in code, and they speak in body language, and the person who is being put down knows. Children know. Children are very sensitive to that kind of thing, and they know when people are looking down on them. I hate that.'

Paula Meehan

Paula Meehan

Fact File

1955 Born in Dublin, the eldest of six children.

STARTED school in England, but soon came back to Ireland and lived a lot of her childhood with her grandparents in inner-city Dublin; later moved to Finglas with her family, but continued to spend time with her grandparents, who by then had moved to Marino.

1972–7 Studied English, history and classical civilisation in Trinity College Dublin (with a year out for travel).

AFTER she left college, Paula went travelling through Europe and especially to Greece, where she wanted to see the sites of the Greek myths that she had loved learning about in Trinity.

1981–3 Studied for a master's degree in poetry-writing at Eastern Washington University.

1984 Had her first book of poetry, *Return and no Blame*, published by Beaver Row Press in Dublin; followed by several other books published in Ireland, the UK and the US over the years.

1996 Elected a member of Aosdána, a community of Ireland's finest writers and artists.

2003 Her play *The Wolf of Winter* was staged by the Abbey Theatre, Dublin; Paula has also written several radio plays broadcast by RTÉ and some of her plays have been published as books; some of her plays are for children and young people.

2013–6 Served as Ireland Professor of Poetry at Trinity College Dublin, UCD and Queen's University Belfast.

2016 *Geomantic* was published in Dublin by Dedalus Press.

Sonia O'Sullivan

born 1969

Sonia O'Sullivan is one of the most successful international Irish female athletes ever

Sonia O'Sullivan won three World Championship gold medals and three European Championship gold medals for middle-distance running. She broke four world records, one of which she still holds. O'Sullivan competed in four Olympic Games over her career and won a silver medal at the Sydney games in 2000.

Sonia was a popular athlete among Irish sports fans. This is partly because of her repeated success, of course, but also because of her spirit and her dedication to her sport. Unlike many other athletes, she has never been involved in any kind of drugs scandal. She has had some bad luck in her career, but she always had the strength of character to put setbacks and conflict behind her and to set her sights on the next challenge.

Her talent developed early and she loved running from a young age. She dedicated herself to her training while still a schoolgirl. When the school day ended at four o'clock in the afternoon, Sonia would go straight to the track and spend an hour training. Then she would go home and study for the rest of the evening. She allowed nothing to divert her from this routine. She wouldn't join her friends at discos at the weekends either,

> Sonia O'Sullivan was famous for her 'kick'. She would hang back for most of the race, but near the end she would suddenly sprint forward and overtake other runners. This was a difficult strategy and it took a lot of intelligence on her part to pull it off. It made her a very exciting runner to watch.

> 'It didn't matter what else was on, rain, sunshine, otherwise, she trained from four till five.'
>
> *John O'Sullivan, Sonia's father*

> 'I used to tell them I wasn't allowed to go, but I really didn't want to go. I was more interested in getting my training done and going to races on the weekend.'
>
> *Sonia O'Sullivan*

preferring to keep herself fit and to attend sports events.

Sonia O'Sullivan won a sports scholarship to an American university, Villanova in Pennsylvania. She studied accountancy and continued to train as an athlete while she studied. She got her degree in 1992, and just after that she took part in her first Olympics, in Barcelona. She came fourth in the 3000-metre final on that occasion, which was quite an achievement, but fourth place meant that she didn't get a medal.

Although Sonia O'Sullivan repeatedly won international championships, Olympic glory evaded her on all but one occasion. She had a bad experience in her second Olympic outing, at the Atlanta games in 1996. She was world champion for 5000 metres at the time and the favourite to win Olympic gold, but she did not finish the final race. Apparently the brand of sportsgear that she was wearing as she was about to run did not comply with the branding rules of the Olympics. For this reason, Sonia was forced to change her running gear just as she was going to run. This had to be upsetting for her at a very pressurised moment,

> 'Nobody died,' said Sonia's dad after this disaster. 'She'll come back. Let her have time, then we'll talk.'

though she herself claimed it did not put her off her stride. The reason she ran so badly, she explained later, was that she was suffering from diarrhoea.

She put that experience behind her and went on to win the silver medal for 5000 metres in the Sydney games in the year

2000. That was the pinnacle of her Olympic success.

She was unfortunate once again at the Athens Olympics in 2004. She came in last in the 5000-metre final, which was devastating for her. Later it emerged that she had had food poisoning. She probably should not have run the race at all, but she was determined to give it her best.

By then she was thirty-four years of age, and Athens was to be her last Olympics, though she did not know that at the time. She tried to qualify for the marathon at the Beijing Olympics in 2008, but that didn't work out for her.

She was more successful in other arenas, notably the World Championships, winning the gold medal for 5000 metres in 1995 and two cross-country gold medals, one each for the long and short courses, in 1998. She also had success in the European Championships, winning gold for 3000 metres in 1994 and gold medals for both 5000 metres and 10,000 metres in 1998.

She broke four world records over her career, and one of these still stands: the outdoor running record for 2000 metres, which she completed in 5:25:36 in 1994.

Sonia O'Sullivan was beaten on various occasions by athletes who, it now seems, took drugs. In particular, there have been

'Sonia has had a bad stomach problem all day and in truth should not have run but this was the Olympic final. She was very sick after the race.'

Nick Bideau, Sonia O'Sullivan's coach, on her failed 5000-metre race in the Athens Olympics 2004

'Without the people from Ireland in the stands, I probably would not have finished the race.'

Sonia O'Sullivan, on the same race

reports in the Chinese media that a team of Chinese athletes who swept the boards in international championships in the 1990s were using drugs. It is possible that Sonia O'Sullivan will be retrospectively awarded at least one and maybe even two gold medals that she was cheated out of by Chinese doping practices when she was at the height of her powers. She has never been embroiled in doping scandals herself.

Sonia O'Sullivan has managed to maintain her career as a competitive runner through two pregnancies and the births of her children, Ciara (born in 1999) and Sophie (born in 2001), at a time when Sonia was winning medals for running. She had to be careful, during her pregnancies, to train at a level that would be safe for her and her unborn child. That worked well for her, and she actually believes that having children gives a female athlete a physical advantage.

'It takes speed to be competitive in individual races, and strength to be able to run back-to-back races in such a competitive environment.

'It's then that you realise that all the 100-mile weeks start to make sense, building strength and endurance through the winter so you don't falter at the championships as you make your way through the rounds.'

Sonia O'Sullivan on running in the World Championships

In the years after the 2004 Olympics, Sonia O'Sullivan began to wind down her career. She ran her last professional competitive race in 2007, when she finished in second place in the 5000 metres at the Woodie's DIY National Senior Track & Field Championships in Santry, Dublin.

She had married her coach, the Australian Nick (or Nic) Bideau, the father of her daughters, in 2006. In that same year she became an Australian citizen. O'Sullivan now lives in Australia with her family. She still considers Ireland home, though, and travels back and forth, often two or three times a year.

She may be retired, but Sonia O'Sullivan has not lost her love for running. She often takes part in runs, many for charity. She was in charge of the Irish team in the London Olympic games in 2012. She has commentated at international athletics championships for RTÉ and she contributes a regular column to *The Irish Times*.

It looks as if Sonia has passed on her talent, her drive and her enthusiasm to her younger daughter: Sophie won two under-17 Australian national titles for running in 2017.

'Ciara was born in July 1999, and I knew in my own mind this left me with just over a year to prepare for the 2000 Sydney Olympics.'

Sonia O'Sullivan

'Motherhood definitely brings its challenges, but it certainly doesn't mean you have to give up your chosen sport. You may just have to do things a bit differently.'

Sonia O'Sullivan

Sonia O'Sullivan

Fact File

1969 Born in Cobh, County Cork.

1992 Graduated from Villanova University, Philadelphia, USA.

1992 Took fourth place in the 3000-metres in her first Olympics, in Barcelona.

1994 Broke the world record for 2000 metres. This record still stands.

1994 European Championship gold medal for 3000 metres.

1995 World Championship gold medal for 5000 metres.

1996 Ran in the 5000-metre final in the Atlanta Olympics but failed to secure a medal.

1998 Won European Championship gold medals for 5000 and 10,000 metres.

1998 Won two World Championship gold medals for long and short cross-country races.

1999 Her daughter Ciara was born.

2000 Took the silver medal in the 5000 metres in the Sydney Olympics.

2000 Won the Dublin Marathon.

2001 Her daughter Sophie was born.

2004 Came a devastating last in the 5000 metres in the Athens Olympics.

2006 Married Nick Bideau, her coach and the father of her daughters.

2006 Became an Australian citizen.

Glossary

Anglican Member of the Church of England, which is the official religion in Britain, or the Church of Ireland, which is a minority Christian religion in Ireland; Anglicans are often called Protestants, but there are some Anglicans who do not consider themselves Protestants

anthropology Study of the culture, especially the rituals and beliefs, of peoples

(Roman) Catholic Member of the (Roman) Catholic church, which includes a large proportion of the world's Christians; the headquarters of the Catholic church are in Rome

civil rights The rights of people to the protection of their state, to have a say in how they are governed and to be treated fairly by their government; these rights are sometimes denied to groups such as women or people from certain cultures or races

Civil War (1922–23) A war between pro- and anti-Treaty forces that followed the Irish War of Independence; a civil war is a war that is fought between people from the same country

contraception Any way of preventing pregnancy

Dáil 'Lower' house of the Irish parliament; the government is part of the Dáil

Easter Rising Armed rebellion against British rule in Ireland that took place at Easter in 1916

hunger strike A refusal to eat, used as a method of protest by prisoners, especially political prisoners

loyalist In Northern Ireland, this has much the same meaning as 'unionist' but tends to be used of more extreme unionists or those in favour of violence

marginalised people People who belong to a group that is not valued by society, such as poor people or minorities

misogynist Person who dislikes or discriminates against women

Modernism A 20th-century experimental movement in the arts whereby reality is not represented realistically

MP Member of Parliament, meaning the British parliament at Westminster in London

nationalist In the past, someone who was in favour of Irish independence from Britain; nowadays someone who is in favour of a united Ireland; similar meaning to 'republican' but tends to be used of people who are against violence

Protestant Member of one of the Christian churches other than the Catholic or Orthodox churches

republican Similar to 'nationalist' but tends to be used more about people who support violence as a way to bring about political change; however, many people who call themselves 'republican' are not in favour of violence

Seanad Irish senate or 'upper' house of the Irish parliament; the Seanad has less power than the Dáil

seanchaí Traditional Irish storyteller

seanchas Folklore and traditional stories

sectarianism Hatred of people who belong to a different religion

socialist Person who believes that the wealth of a country should be shared out fairly by the state among all the people; socialist thinking is sometimes called 'left wing'

senator Member of the Seanad

suffrage The right to vote (often refers to women's right to vote)

suffragette Woman who actively fought for women's right to vote in the early 20th century

suffragist Person who supports the right (usually of women or minorities) to vote

Taoiseach Irish prime minister, the most important person in the government

TD Teachta Dála, member of the Dáil, Irish equivalent of MP

trade union Organisation of workers that defends their employment rights

Troubles A period of violent conflict in Northern Ireland from the late 1960s until the mid-1990s

unionist Person who is in favour of Northern Ireland remaining part of the United Kingdom; when it is spelt with a capital U, it often refers to one of the Unionist political parties in Northern Ireland

War of Independence (1919–21) A war against British rule in Ireland, which ended with the controversial Anglo-Irish Treaty, which in turn led to the Civil War

Westminster Literally the place in London where the British parliament sits, but usually it is used to mean the parliament itself

Acknowledgements

The extract from Vona Groarke's translation of 'Caoineadh Airt Uí Laoghaire' is © Vona Groarke. The translation is called *Lament for Art O'Leary* and was published by The Gallery Press, Oldcastle, in 2008. It is reprinted here by kind permission of The Gallery Press.

The extract from Brendan Kennelly's translation of 'Caoineadh Airt Uí Laoghaire' is © Brendan Kennelly. The translation is called 'A Cry for Art O'Leary' from *Love of Ireland: Poems from the Irish*, published by Mercier Press, Cork, in 1989. It is reprinted here by kind permission of the poet.

'The Quilt' is © Paula Meehan. It was included in the book *Geomantic*, published by Dedalus Press, Dublin, in 2016. It is reprinted here by kind permission of the poet and the publisher.

Most of the illustrations in this book are based on photographs. Every effort has been made to trace the copyright holders and obtain permission to reproduce this material. Please do get in touch with any enquiries or any information relating to these images or the rights holders.

The illustration of Anne Devlin is produced with permission of Wicklow County Council Library Service.

The illustration of Augusta, Lady Gregory is produced with permission of Getty Images.

The illustration of Dorothy Stopford-Price is produced by permission of the Royal College of Physicians of Ireland.

The illustrations of Sr Stanislaus Kennedy and Paula Meehan are produced by permission of Radio Teilifís Éireann.

The illustration of Bernadette Devlin McAliskey is produced by permission of the Press Association.

The illustration of Sonia O'Sullivan is produced by permission of Brendan Moran and Sportsfile.

The illustration of Garry Hynes is produced by permission of Keith Pattison.

The illustration of Hannah Sheehy Skeffington is produced by permission of the Sheehy Skeffington family.

The illustration of Peig Sayers is produced by permission of Cnuasach Bhéaloideas Éireann / National Folklore Collection.

The illustration of Lelia Doolan is produced courtesy of Lelia Doolan.

The illustration of Mary Robinson is produced by permission of David De Jonge.

The illustration of Constance Markievicz is produced by permission of the National Library of Ireland.

About the Author

Siobhán Parkinson is a novelist and was Ireland's first laureate for children's literature, Laureate na nÓg (2010–12). She is also a publisher and a translator. Her most recent novel for children is *Miraculous Miranda*, and her latest translation, *Wherever it is Summer* (written in German by Tamara Bach under the title *Was vom Sommer übrig ist*) was IBBY Ireland's Honour Book for Translation in 2017.

This book is her first non-fiction title.

About the Publisher

Based in Dublin, Little Island Books has been publishing books for children and teenagers since 2010. It is Ireland's only English-language publisher that publishes exclusively for young people. Little Island specialises in publishing new Irish writers and illustrators, and also has a commitment to publishing books in translation.

Little
Island